Star Child

Stephen Shaw

Star Child

Stephen Shaw's Books

Visit the website: www.i-am-stephen-shaw.com

I Am contains spiritual and mystical teachings from enlightened masters that point the way to love, peace, bliss, freedom and spiritual awakening.

Heart Song takes you on a mystical adventure into creating your reality and manifesting your dreams, and reveals the secrets to attaining a fulfilled and joyful life.

They Walk Among Us is a love story spanning two realities. Explore the mystery of the angels. Discover the secrets of Love Whispering.

The Other Side explores the most fundamental question in each reality. What happens when the physical body dies? Where do you go? Expand your awareness. Journey deep into the Mystery.

Reflections offers mystical words for guidance, meditation and contemplation. Open the book anywhere and unwrap your daily inspiration.

5D is the Fifth Dimension. Discover ethereal doorways hidden in the fabric of space-time. Seek the advanced mystical teachings.

Star Child offers an exciting glimpse into the future on earth. The return of the gods and the advanced mystical teachings. And the ultimate battle of light versus darkness.

The Tribe expounds the joyful creation of new Earth. What happened after the legendary battle of Machu Picchu? What is Christ consciousness? What is Ecstatic Tantra?

The Fractal Key reveals the secrets of the shamans. This handbook for psychonauts discloses the techniques and practices used in psychedelic healing and transcendent journeys.

My name is Adam. I am an archaeologist researching an unusual place in the Sahara Desert. It goes by the name of Crystal Mountain.

At university they taught us the boring but necessary stuff. For example, the Sahara Desert is the world's largest hot desert. Yes, 'hot desert', as Antarctica and the Arctic are also considered deserts. The Sahara spans over 9,400,000 square kilometres and covers most of North Africa; some of the sand dunes reach 180 metres in height.

The Sahara Desert is in fact a combination of deserts which flow into each other. My interest lies in the ancient White Desert in northern Egypt, situated halfway between Bahariya Oasis and Farafra Oasis. This is where Crystal Mountain is located – a glittering and fascinating mix of rock formations and crystals.

It has been another searing day and I am baked in dust and sweat. My trustworthy old 4x4 is ferrying me back in the dusky light. The prospect of a cool shower and a warm meal fills my mind and helps me focus on driving. In the distance some grey clouds are forming. I notice the temperature is dropping rapidly. Unusual. It never rains here.

The sky darkens. Suddenly I am immersed in a torrential storm. Jump out, try to put the roof up. A powerful gust rips it from my hands. Squatting beside the vehicle for protection. Lightning streaks hard into the ground, the flash blinding me for a moment. The smell of fresh rain and fire. A deafening noise. I cover my ears and struggle to see what's happening. Is that a giant hawk?

When I awaken, it is calm and still. The sky is clear and the stars are glistening. I blink a few times. The white sand seems especially bright … perhaps there is a full moon … or maybe it is the reflection of the headlights.

Here, let me give you a hand. A glowing naked man is standing before me. Adrenaline kicks in. My arm brushes against the knife at my side. "Who are you? What do you want?"

He smiles. *A pair of trousers would be nice.*

I reach into the 4x4 and throw him my spare khaki trousers. A long-sleeve white shirt follows. I wait until he is dressed, then "What do you want? Where did you come from?"

My name is Ra. He points to the sky. *I travelled from the sun.*

Great. Lost and deranged. "Adam Kadmon. Get in the car. You can't stay out here. Keep your hands where I can see them."

On the way back he talks incessantly. *What year is it?* "2023, June" *It's been a long time … Where do you live?* "Italy" *What do you do?* "Research ancient relics" *Why are you out here?* "Searching for a crystal that can handle advancing nanotechnology." *Nanotechnology?* "Um, a crystal able to hold and transmit pulses of light to transfer and store digital information as quantum bits."

I sigh inwardly. What am I supposed to say? Just keep him occupied until he is unloaded somewhere safe. *Are you transferring information onto light beams utilizing the natural nuclear spin of photons in a laser beam?* My foot hits the brake hard. I wipe the sweat from my brow. "Ok, who are you? And why are you exuding such heat? It feels like midday in here!"

I am Ra, the sun-god, the god of light. I entered earth through a one-way portal, rendering me naked and vulnerable in your reality. I risked it all to fulfil a prophecy, to bring a new age of peace to your planet.

2

Holding the steering wheel tightly, I gaze sympathetically at him. "You need help, my friend."

Do you have a portable electronic information device?

I pull the lume from my pocket. It's wafer-thin, 12 by 6 centimetres, and weighs almost nothing. One touch and a holographic image pops up. The female voice says "Hi Adam, what can I do for you today?"

Ra smiles and points at my communication device. Instantly a beam of light emanates from his finger and the lume displays a picture of a glowing hawk-headed man in a white robe. He carries a staff by his side. *That's me, the god of light. Ra means 'sun' or 'creative power'. I used to spend time in Lunu, Place of Pillars, also known as City of the Sun, in Egypt. In a sense, I am returning home.* Fleeting images rise and fall on my lume: the lands of ancient Egypt; the building of the pyramids; ceremonies in sacred temples; powerful weapons and communication devices; and the mythological figures of Geb and Nut and their children Osiris, Isis, Seth and Nephthys.

"How are you doing this?"

Information is stored in quantum packets of light. Why should there be any barriers in light communication?

"If you are from the ancient past, why are you more advanced than us?"

We originate from the stars. The gods gradually left your planet about 2,000 years ago. Our advanced teachings slowly disappeared because of humankind's selfishness, greed and war. It's an age-old lesson. Leave a people to take responsibility for themselves and their planet, leave a people to autonomously determine their own destiny, and what happens? Priests are supposed to teach presence, acceptance, loving-kindness and awareness of the multi-dimensions. Leaders are supposed to ensure equitable distribution of jobs and wealth, respect of cultural differences and freedom of expression. But power is now concentrated in the hands of a few souls – the dark masters who control worldwide political, economic, religious and media power. And the masses are beautifully confined within this invisible dark lattice.

"What the hell are you talking about?"

Adam Kadmon, do you believe you are free? Do you truly believe you live in a democracy? Do you have a voice? Do you have a say in your political and economic strategy?

I look at him thoughtfully. Maybe he is crazy after all. Who can challenge the overwhelming voice of the media? The media that reports only the messages and ideology of those in power? We vote for one puppet after another and the world is still in economic chaos. Entire countries are now debt slaves. One fifth of the world's population is poor and starving, yet it is seldom mentioned in the newsfeed. When I think about it with my full attention it just makes me feel hopeless and a bit depressed.

I am here to bring change to your planet. But I cannot do it alone. Our paths crossed for a reason. I need your help.

"What are you asking me to do?"

To share in the greatest journey you can imagine. To risk everything for something beyond yourself.

"When do you need an answer?"

Now is a really good time.

"Oh."

* * *

4

I start the engine and let it idle for a while. My brow furrows. I have always had this feeling that there is more to this earth than meets the eye, more to life than what history tells us. All those myths and mysteries – there has to be some substance to them. And now this opportunity thrown across my path. Destiny? Random chance?

I remember reading a book called Heart Song a few years ago. What was it the author wrote? Ah, yes. '... *true opportunities come across your path infrequently. Notice when something or someone connects deeply with your soul. Choose carefully and follow your heart. The wise person seizes those opportunities.*' Perhaps this is one of those rare moments.

I look at Ra. I have no idea who this guy is, but what he did with that light beam is not possible. At least in my world. "I'll take the chance. I'll do it."

The glowing bald-headed man with luminous blue eyes nods solemnly. *Thank you.* A brief pause. *By the way, I have a cat.*

"Excuse me?"

My faithful companion, Baset, on the back seat.

I turn around. Twinkling green eyes stare at me from a perfectly relaxed position. Been sitting there all along. I take a deep breath. "From the sun too?"

Of course. Baset is the protector and defender of Ra. She is known as the Lady of Flame and Eye of Ra.

"Hmm, got the first name ... but Eye of Ra?"

Her all-seeing eye perceives everything, everywhere, in every dimension.

"In every dimension?"

There are many dimensions. You are focusing your consciousness in just one or two. Baset is not limited in the same way.

Why do those words sound so familiar? Are they from another book I have read?

You are an expression of Life. You exist across many dimensions. In fact, you exist across all dimensions.

My mind drifts to my academic studies. Cats in ancient Egypt were sacred and respected animals. They were highly revered because of their ability to eliminate rats and mice, which threatened food supplies, and their ability to combat snakes. Although the ancient Egyptians were the first to domesticate cats, they often took them on hunting trips. Statues of cats were also placed outside buildings to protect occupants and ward off evil spirits. I guess they had some sort of spiritual significance.

I glance at Baset again. She looks harmless enough – bronze, short-haired, purring away on an old blanket. Such intense green eyes. I engage the gear and start driving.

"Is she an Egyptian Mau?"

Indeed. Well spotted.

Egyptian Maus are easily identified by the scarab beetle or M marking on their foreheads and by the long dark stripe that runs along the spine from head to tail. Sleek and muscular, they are the fastest of the domestic cats and reach speeds of over 58 km/h. Maus are a relatively rare breed, well known for their intelligence, close bonding and unusual musical voices.

Ra and Baset soon slip into a quiet slumber, leaving me alone with my thoughts. It feels peaceful in the car and before long

I see the familiar outline of palm trees. A warm shower, a late dinner and a soft bed for each of us. I wonder what tomorrow will bring.

* * *

Italy! We have to go to Italy!

Ra, bursting in all excited, snaps me back to reality. I put down my breakfast pita. For a brief moment I had forgotten about the events of yesterday. And my commitment.

Baset has spent the night scanning for the location of my staff. She has found it! We need to go to Italy!

I sigh. What have I gotten myself into? "Doesn't she sleep?" I run my fingers through my hair. Perhaps cats are naturally nocturnal. "What staff?"

The Staff of Light. I passed it to Osiris when I left for other realms. It has been carefully handed down in sacred ceremonies for thousands of years.

"The one you were holding in the picture on my lume? Silver-white colour, pine cone at the top, and two serpents intertwined along it?"

That's the one.

"What's so special about this staff?"

It focuses the light. Light can be used as a weapon; it can be used to communicate with other realms; and it can open the consciousness to the multi-dimensions.

"Ah. That's cleared that up then. Where may we find this wonderful device?"

It is located in the Court of the Pine Cone, Vatican City.

"The Cortile della Pigna? Where that huge bronze pine cone statue is displayed? Are you crazy? Vatican City is a sovereign independent state locked safely behind huge walls within the city of Rome. And it is sacred to a vast number of Catholics."

There is something much bigger at stake than religiosity. The fate of the people of this world depends on how we act now.

I wonder if all the gods are so dramatic. I scratch my head. "Um … ordinary citizens can attend tours of the Vatican. You are allowed to walk into the Cortile della Pigna. Where exactly is the staff?"

Hidden just beneath the pine cone statue. In a channel too narrow for a human to access.

"Perfect. So we join a tour, somehow extract an inaccessible staff and then miraculously walk out unnoticed."

My plan exactly. Baset will play an important part.

"Your plan, your responsibility. I know someone currently docking in Porto Marina, Alexandria, just north of here. I'll make the call. If we're lucky he will give us a ride to the Tevere Yacht Club, Porto Romano, just outside Rome."

Thank you.

I finish breakfast and wander off to phone Xavier, a long-time friend who regularly transports yachts across the world. When I return, I have good news for Ra. "We leave first thing tomorrow morning. I will book us onto the latest tour of the day. The rest is up to you. I am going to Crystal Mountain now. See you later."

Baset is purring like a lioness while curling affectionately around Ra's legs. He waves a quick goodbye. I jump in the 4x4 and prepare to do what I love the most. In glorious peace and solitude.

* * *

The next morning is an early start. Ra seems unusually quiet during the drive. Baset is asleep on his lap. We reach Porto Marina in good time. Xavier is staying in the resort and has organised a space for the 4x4. The parking of the car startles both companions into full wakefulness.

We stroll across to the harbour and soon find Xavier, all tanned and smiling, washing down a glistening white yacht. I give him a hug and a firm pat on the back. "Good to see you, mate! How are you? How is your gorgeous woman?"

His cyan eyes twinkle in the light: "Life couldn't be better. Zara is thriving in Bimini. It's all good."

I introduce Ra and the cat. "Thanks for the favour. I hope it's not out of your way."

"Not at all. I am meeting another old friend from Florence later. We're having dinner at the yacht club in Porto Romano. The boat will be docked overnight. If you need a ride back to Alexandria just make sure you are on board by eight in the morning."

Once we set sail Ra comes alive with conversation. He is chatting with Xavier. I can hear snippets about "fire-beings and water-beings" and quickly lose interest. The sea is a little choppy but the sky is clear and blue. I breathe in the fresh invigorating air.

There is nothing like being out on the open water. So much nature everywhere.

I adore the quiet and solitude. I am sitting on the bow of the yacht staring at the hypnotic waves. Baset comes trundling along, seats herself next to me and gazes at the surging ripples. The ambience shifts into remarkable stillness ... it's the strangest feeling ... almost as if we are kindred spirits travelling in another dimension.

The reverie is broken by our arrival. "Give me a hand with the ropes, please." We moor the boat and disembark. I have a long stretch, tell Xavier we'll see him later and then head off to find the bus to Rome. My heart suddenly starts beating faster – we have a strange and unpredictable day ahead of us!

The Vatican City tour is booked for the afternoon so the morning is spent absorbing classic Roman landmarks. We visit the Colosseum on Piazza del Colosseo; appraise the architecture of the ancient Pantheon; throw a coin into the Trevi Fountain; and walk through the gardens of the Villa Borghese. Delicious thin-crust pizzas made in a wood-fired oven add the finishing touch. Baset enjoys a plate of grilled sardines. It seems that even gods need to eat.

"Hope your cat is going to become invisible," I say as we enter Vatican City.

Ra nods sagely. *Don't worry, she can take care of herself.*

Our tour begins in St Peter's Basilica, the largest church in Christianity, guardian of St Peter's tomb, Michelangelo's Pieta sculpture and Bernini's immense baldachin canopy. Afterward we explore the Vatican Museum, which comprises over 14 kilometres and 2,000 rooms of classic artwork. We revere the sculptures in the Gallery of Statues; delight in the works of Raphael in the Raphael Rooms; admire the paintings of Caravaggio, Leonardo da Vinci, Fra Angelico, Giotto, Poussin and Titian; and savour Michelangelo's astounding frescoes The Creation of Adam and The Last Judgement in the Sistine Chapel.

Later we amble to the Cortile della Pigna. It is a huge square divided into four manicured lawns with various sculptures. There it is! The four-metre-high bronze pine cone with a peacock on either side and a fountain beneath. Quite marvellous to behold.

It is twilight. Ra motions for us to sit on the grass verge. *Are you aware of the significance of this statue? Do you understand the symbolism before you?*

"The pine cone was prevalent in ancient art and architecture. The symbol has been found in the ruins of the Indonesians, Babylonians, Egyptians, Greeks, Romans and Christians. It also appears in the drawings of esoteric traditions like Freemasonry, Theosophy, Gnosticism and esoteric Christianity. Not sure I understand what it means though."

The pine cone symbolises the spiritual third eye and its physical counterpart the pineal gland. The shape of the pineal gland resembles a tiny pine cone and it is buried deep in the centre of the brain between the two hemispheres. The pine cone therefore refers to awakening, to enlightenment, to the consciousness entering the multi-dimensions, to accessing the hidden knowledge, to embracing the Light.

"Wow. That is a little different to archaeology."

The water flowing beneath the statue represents the flow of Life, the flow of creation. The manifestation of the unmanifested Creative Life Force.

"Um, ok …"

The peacocks represent the myriad possibilities of Life, the innumerable expressions of the I Am. When the peacocks splay their feathers, what do you see? A multitude of eyes symbolising the hidden multi-dimensions.

Ra puts his hand on my shoulder and gazes at me.

The greatest truth you will ever know is that Life is breathing. In this very moment, in the Now, there is a simultaneous In-Breath and Out-Breath.

I look at him quizzically.

The Source manifests countless dimensions and infinite realities – the Out-Breath, the act of creation. And all of creation flows back to the Source – the In-Breath, the return and dissolution. This is the flow of Life.

Before I can comment, a pair of green eyes flashes from the shadows. It is Baset, standing over the sparkling Staff of Light. Ra hurries over excitedly, mutters a few words of gratitude and then raises the staff high in the air. Twelve lightning bolts streak from the pine cone into the heavens. He slams the base of the staff into the ground and shouts exuberantly: *And so it begins!*

Great. So much for a discreet exit. Now I have a sun-god, a magical staff and a cat to escort from the city. There are security cameras everywhere. How shall I describe the ensuing events? A heart-pounding rush to the gate; being chased down the streets by the Swiss Guard; hailing a taxi while holding a screeching Mau; a swift run to the harbour; then hiding quietly within the unlit yacht.

I phone Xavier and suggest that leaving tonight would be a really good idea. An hour later we set sail under a moonless sky. I breathe a sigh of relief. We have just escaped from the smallest country in the world.

* * *

Xavier hastily departs for Florida the next morning while I bundle my compatriots into the 4x4. No amount of glaring will induce any contrition in Ra, who now sits quietly in the back seat. I am wondering about the possible consequences of our actions. Interestingly, there is nothing in the newsfeed. Nothing at all. It's kind of ominous.

I glance at Ra in the mirror. "Why are the authorities not reporting what happened?"

They are not the ones in charge. There is a bigger agenda now. The 42-month countdown has begun.

"What countdown?"

Did I not tell you about Apophis?

"Who?"

It's a long story. After breakfast let's go to Crystal Mountain and I will tell you everything.

I heave a sigh. It's tempting to walk away; instead I grit my teeth and honour my commitment. "Alright, let's grab a shower and something to eat. Meet me back at the vehicle in forty-five minutes."

The sun is high by the time we get to Crystal Mountain. July is a scorching time of year. The moment we arrive, Baset alights and races away with astonishing speed. I wonder if all Maus move so swiftly.

Ra accompanies me to the dig. For the first hour I am able to focus on my work, but it is obvious that he desperately wants to talk. Finally I relent: "Ok, tell me about Apophis."

He sits down near me and begins making small circles in the sand.

Apep, as he was originally called, arrived on earth a short time after me. He was also a star traveller. I welcomed his arrival, as I saw the opportunity to combine our forces to benefit your planet. During the first years we worked in harmony, bringing advanced teachings on architecture, construction, agriculture, mathematics and writing. We shared our knowledge and some of our technology.

Over time it became clear that Apep enjoyed power. He and his entourage began systematically oppressing and dominating the native population. He renamed himself Apophis, proclaimed himself the god of darkness, and demanded that he be worshipped. He regularly shape-shifted into the form of a tall lizard, earning him the epithet Dark Lizard or Evil Lizard.

A war in the heavens ensued. Our superior technology ensured that most of Apophis' airships were destroyed. Sadly, many humans died too. Apophis, his deputies Sek and Mot, and the remaining dark ones, as they had come to be known, disappeared and never returned.

"A great success. Who fought on your side?"

The nine gods of light: Hathor, Shu, Tefnut, Geb, Nut, Osiris, Isis, Seth and Nephthys.

"Where did they come from?"

I created them.

"Oh ..."

After the battle with Apophis I despatched the gods to spread the advanced teachings throughout the planet. Whenever they arrived in a new country they adopted a local name to blend with the populace. The gods, of course, had a natural tendency to lead and rule. Many became kings and rulers, shaping entire cultures in their image. We eventually understood that godly leaders and priests create disempowered and dependent peoples who no longer embrace autonomy and responsibility nor progress spiritually. So we concealed some of our technology at sacred sites and gradually withdrew from the earth.

"Hence all the myths and mysteries in our history ..."

Before we left the earth the nine gods procreated two children of light. They were directed to stay on this planet until our return. Their mission was to watch over humankind, intervening only when absolutely necessary. They have been here all this time, working quietly and in secret.

One of the Watchers tended to be solitary and reclusive, forging an intimate bond with the natural world. We called her the Guardian of the Earth. The other tends to connect more with humankind, keeping a close eye on genetic codes, advancing technology and politico-socio-economic systems. He is known as the Star Child.

"Is this leading to the prophecy you mentioned when we first met?"

Indeed. Isis was a remarkable seer who predicted the return of Apophis to this planet. She foresaw a similar cycle of events – this time a 42-month rise to power and popularity followed by a 42-month reign of darkness. She foretold that I would return to earth at the beginning of this 7-year cycle.

"I gather that Apophis is back?"

He returned many years ago, initially living a quiet life in Libya, north Africa. The Guardian of the Earth positioned herself in Ethiopia to watch for developments. In 2017 he grabbed power and became the leader of a Middle Eastern country. The Guardian foolishly tried to battle him alone, hurling the four elementals and despatching ferocious animals to hunt and destroy him. She succeeded only in seriously wounding him and he now bears a visible scar on his head. Unfortunately her life was ended.

Ra looks away and stares into the distance. My mind is raking through previous newsfeeds. Which Middle Eastern country? Who carries such a visible scar? How come I never heard about this important skirmish?

Baset comes screeching around the rock formation, making me jump. What is it with her?

She has found what she was seeking. Will you come with me?

We follow the Mau to one of the distant archways, halting before an obscure sub-volcanic cave. I crouch and inspect the entrance. There is a short crawl-space then it widens out. I hate these tight spaces. This better be worth it. Once inside, I pull the pointed trowel from my pocket and scrape the wall. A faded glimmer. I gouge out some of the stones. Rough diamonds!

"Unbelievable. Is this what you wanted to show me?"

Stay here and collect as many as possible. You are going to need those stones for currency.

"What?"

Once Apophis finds out who you are, he will send the dark ones after you. You will no longer be able to use electronic currency or any electronic device registered under your name. It makes it too easy to track you.

"What are you talking about?"

Ra appears surprised. *Have you forgotten your promise? To risk everything for something beyond yourself?*

I am quiet for a few moments. Is this actually happening? Are there events on this earth that no one reports? Are there dark puppet-masters pulling our strings and making us dance to invisible tunes? What realities are hidden from our world?

He exits the cave, leaving me to excavate my future. I spend the rest of the afternoon diligently poking and sifting through the dirt, trying to make sense of my life. A life that appears to be spiralling rapidly out of control.

On the way back a pensive mood imbues the 4x4. I guess we both have a lot to contemplate. After dinner I sit outside and stare at the desert. Tomorrow I need to ask Ra some important questions.

* * *

The only way to defeat the darkness is to unite the light on this earth.

It's a bit early for a lecture but I need some knowledge before I can proceed. Feel way out of my depth and far beyond my comfort zones.

"What is it you plan to do? And how am I involved?"

I intend to defeat Apophis and spread light on your planet. People are tired of living in darkness. Everyone desires to be free, to have a voice, to find peace and happiness. This world has to change. Poverty and hunger have to end. Environmental damage and pollution can no longer continue unabated. Wars must cease. Loving-kindness and responsibility need to return to this world.

"What has this to do with me?"

You have an eye for exploration and discovery. There are sacred relics hidden around this planet which we need to find.

"Oh."

Top of the list is the Adi Shakti. It's in India.

"India? What about my work here?"

Adam, you now have a mission. It's time to serve your planet.

"Do I have a choice?"

Ra smiles knowingly. *You always have a choice.*

"I need some time to think. I enjoy my work. I didn't ask for this mission."

He nods respectfully. *I understand.*

I get up, pat him on the shoulder and walk to the 4x4. A few days in the desert will sort this out.

* * *

My life is returning to relative normality. Peace, solitude, sweat, scraping, brushing and dusting. It gives me plenty of time to reflect and ponder upon the recent events.

The deluge of spiritual and political information has left me reeling. I am trying to process everything he has said. There is probably more I can learn from the sun-god, especially in the areas of archaeology and history. Maybe I am missing an opportunity.

The Vatican escapade streams into my mind. Is that what my life will be like? A series of scary and exhilarating adventures? Do I need to grow up? I am collecting more rough diamonds to keep my options open. Ra's words have gotten under my skin. *To risk everything for something beyond yourself.*

The ground is being rapidly overshadowed. Strange. There is not a cloud in the sky. The faint sound of shifting gravel. I wipe the sweat from my brow and scan the distant rock formation. A dark figure is crouching by the boulder. An unusual fear courses through my body.

I slip under the archway and try to calm myself. This is a ridiculous reaction. I am alone in the desert. The warm air is causing a mirage. Suddenly a light beam is fired toward me. What the hell is happening?

A small creature streaks past. Carefully, I peek around the corner. It's Baset! Blurring through the air with a ferocious high-pitched screech, then a fierce tangle of claws and fangs. I shiver involuntarily. Moments later she is purring beside me.

We jump in the 4x4 and make a rapid departure. I have no idea what just happened. What was Baset doing in the desert? My thoughts are racing. I drive furiously.

Ra is sitting under a palm tree. *You're just in time! Have you seen the newsfeed?*

Before I can speak he holds out his hands and displays a holographic image:

'Today marks the establishment of the World Peace Organisation. The founder and leader of this organisation is a charismatic and eccentric politician from the Middle East, a man who says that he no longer wishes to have an official title but will now simply be known as Apophis. At its inception the World Peace Organisation includes most of Europe, the Middle East and Africa. Apophis has stated that the WPO will work toward world peace and unity, and strive to eradicate poverty and hunger.'

"Looks like he has put you out of a job."

Did you notice the significance of today's date? 7 July 2023.

I shrug. "All 7's? The official beginning of the 42-month cycle?"

Exactly. The Dark Lizard is going to look like a saint for the rest of this year and through 2024, 25 and 26. Everything will shift in 2027 when the second 42-month cycle commences.

The newsfeed is displaying a picture of Apophis. Oh, it's him! I scrutinise his face, trying hard to memorise his features. Then Ra closes his hands and the images disappear.

"How did you do that? You are not using an electronic device."

Light can be the medium and the message. Light is the core of many of your future technologies.

Baset curls around Ra's legs, staring him directly in the eyes. The sun-god looks up at me. He knows about the desert incident.

It is no longer safe for you to be here. Book a flight to Punjab, India. I will meet you there. This may be the last time you will be able to pay electronically.

I swallow hard, extract my lume and touch the activator. Trying to keep my voice steady, I issue a command: "Book a flight!"

* * *

Having never been to India before, my expectations are somewhat removed from reality. According to the flight magazine: 'Punjab is located in northwest India and its name means Land of Five Rivers. It is one of the best places to live in India, as it affords a high quality of life to its residents and has the lowest level of hunger in the country. It is a very fertile region, ideal for growing wheat, rice, cotton, sugar cane, fruits and vegetables. Punjab is often called the Granary of India or India's bread-basket, as it produces a high percentage of India's wheat and rice.'

Ra is waiting for me outside Amritsar airport. We have arrived in the monsoon season, perfect timing if you enjoy heavy rain and high humidity. *We need to keep a low profile for a while so this will be our home for a few months. Did you bring the diamonds?*

"Finances are going to be the least of our worries. What's the game plan?"

I hope you are a patient man, Adam Kadmon. We have a 7-year cycle ahead of us. There are many unpredictable elements. Much to explore and learn. Our number one priority is to stay alive.

"Seriously?"

Yes. The dark ones know about us. We have moved onto their radar. They are aware of the prophecy and will be hunting us.

"I am never going back to my old life, am I?"

It is unlikely. Perhaps there is a better life waiting for you.

A car pulls up alongside and "Sat Sri Akal!" erupts from a white-robed man wearing a turban. Ra places his palms together in front of his chest and bows lightly. *Blessed is the person who says God is Truth!*

"Hey Ra, how you doing?"

Good, thank you. This is my friend Adam. He is part of our wonderful adventure. Adam, this is Sikh Nanak. He is a member of the Council of Light and will be looking after us.

21

"Greetings, Adam!"

I follow the same protocol as Ra. Another piece of the mystery unfolds before me.

We bundle into the car and the effervescent Sikh brings me up to date: "About 60% of the people in Punjab are Sikhs and around 35% are Hindus. The latter greet with a 'Namaste'. Our turbans signal that we live in the image of Infinity and are dedicated to serving all."

"And the Council of Light?"

The Sikh glances at Ra, who nods his approval. "The Council was set up to counter the force of evil through the power of prayer, meditation, chanting and other religious practices. We direct vast amounts of positive energy to the people of this planet. We are not gods, however, and all we are doing is bringing balance to our world. Since Apophis arrived there has been a huge surge in the dark force, more than we can handle alone."

Hence our mission, Adam.

"Yes, I understand. How many people make up this Council?"

Twelve. Selected because of their unconditional unwavering commitment to light, love and truth. They also need to be leaders of their religious order or tribe.

"Well then, I am honoured to be in such company." I smile broadly at the Sikh.

"Thank you." He bows his head reverently.

Where are we headed, my good friend?

"Your home will be within walking distance of our holiest of shrines, the Sri Harmandir Sahib or Golden Temple, right here in Amritsar. Do you know what Amritsar means? Holy Pool of Nectar. It's such a beautiful description for our city."

After an hour of unpacking and settling in, I join the others for dinner. It is not long before I excuse myself to retire for the night. My head relaxes on the soft pillow. There is a lot to think about but I am asleep within minutes.

* * *

Sikh Nanak is making the short walk from our home to the temple. "So what is the Adi Shakti? It is the symbol of our religion: Two swords of protection surrounding the circle of creation, all balancing on the double-edged sword of cause and effect. However, few people know that the Adi Shakti actually exists. It was originally a gift from the goddess Shakti. It is a powerful sacred relic securely concealed in the Golden Temple."

"I am not familiar with the goddess Shakti."

"Adi means 'primordial' and Shakti means 'power'. So Adi Shakti means Primordial Power of God. There exists nothing but God and his Shakti. God is the unmanifested observer and she is the embodiment of his dreams. She creates all the universes with her endless love. She in fact *is* the creation. All of creation is merely a beautiful cloak to wrap God in and make him visible."

Wow. I will need to ponder that over the next few days.

We round a corner and find a temple gate. Everyone is requested to remove their shoes, store them at the place provided and wash their feet before entering the premises. Bare feet and a light head-covering are the order of the day. We cross the threshold and are greeted by the most spectacular sight: An enormous white temple complex encompassing a still lake, upon which floats a magnificent golden building.

The Sikh continues. "The entire temple complex is called the Golden Temple even though the golden building is only one part of it. Anyone may enter the complex irrespective of religion, colour, creed or gender. The four entrances symbolise acceptance and openness. Every day of the year free vegetarian meals are served to tens of thousands of people in the Guru Ka Langar or community kitchen. The majority of the temple work is done by volunteers."

We are not even charged an entrance fee. What a marvellous and truly spiritual place.

"The most famous and holy part of our temple is the Hari Mandir or Divine Temple – that beautiful golden structure surrounded by the sacred Amrit Sarovar or Pool of Nectar. The pathway that connects to the Divine Temple is a marble causeway called Guru's Bridge. The Divine Temple enshrines the holy book, Guru Granth Sahib, which is venerated by pilgrims from all over the world. It also conceals the Adi Shakti."

Ra stretches his arms expansively. *What a glorious and breathtaking sacred site!*

We take a leisurely stroll along the marble concourse encircling the lake and slowly make our way to Guru's Bridge. The Divine Temple is constructed from white and gold-plated marble, and the walls are encrusted with precious stones and decorated with verses from the Sikh holy book. We reach the top floor and sit quietly for a while.

A weird feeling comes over me. Suddenly the words pour out: "Sikh Nanak, I wish to stay and learn the Sikh philosophy. Here is something that is quite beautiful and free and true, something I wish to understand. Will you mentor me?"

He looks at Ra. "Do we have time?"

Plenty of it. I need to investigate Apophis' technological capabilities and discover his strategy. Rash action will only lead to our demise.

"Are we somehow limited to the prophecy's 7-year cycle?"

A prophecy is like time-travel. It will stupefy you if you contemplate it too deeply. You kind of have to ignore it, do your research and take the action you believe is appropriate. My experience has taught me that there is a measure of free will and flexibility within a prophecy. I have also learned that the words will play out no matter what action I take. It is one of those strange mysteries in life.

"That's really interesting. It reminds of a curious dichotomy. I have this sense of divine guidance and a plan for my life, mingled with the freedom to create my life in whatever way I choose. Yet no matter what I create, I have this idea that something mildly predestined is unfolding. I have never understood this paradoxical mix of my will, dreams and desires and this feeling that there is some orchestration in the background."

Now you are describing every person's life. You are expressed over many dimensions, though your awareness is currently limited to this reality. There are moments when your awareness shifts to encompass other realities. At those times you hear the whispers of the spiritual guardians and connect with your other-dimensional selves. Each level of expanded awareness brings a heightened understanding but also another veil. It can take a lifetime, indeed many lifetimes, to penetrate the veils of the Mystery.

Sikh Nanak speaks: "This is Shakti mentioned earlier. She is infinite. If you swim in her holy waters, you will be lost and found, lost and found, lost and found. It is an adventure with no end. Until you reunite with God."

I am starting to realise that I know nothing. Who knew such Truth was hidden within religion? It will take me years of learning and reflecting to even begin to understand it all.

Ra puts his hand on my shoulder and smiles. *There are quicker ways to awakening and enlightenment. It's called Full Immersion. Direct experience of the Divine. However, learning and reflection are an inescapable part of every spiritual journey.*

"Before you leave, shall I show Adam the Adi Shakti?"

He nods. *Please do.*

The Sikh leads us into a secret chamber hidden behind a wall. Gleaming in the corner are a pair of swords, a circle and another sword. All melded into one unit. "This is an energy shield. It works like this. Touch the left sword to activate, the right to deactivate." He hands it over to me.

The Adi Shakti is quite heavy. I hold it at chest height and touch the left sword. Immediately Ra takes out a large knife and throws it at me. Caught off guard, I am unable to react. The knife ricochets to the side.

"Are you crazy?" I yell. "What do you think you're doing?"

Just making sure it works. You'll need this for your protection.

"How did you know it was activated? The shield is invisible."

Of course it's invisible. Do you not feel the activation?

"Hmm … yes, now that I am less shocked. Great device but unwieldy."

"Adam, press on the circle once."

I do it and the object shrinks to fit into my palm.

"Here is the necklace. Feed it through the top loop of the Adi Shakti. Oh, one more thing – touch the centre sword."

Can you hear me, Adam?

I jump. "Um, yes, I can hear you. This acts as a communication device?"

Indeed.

"Does it have the capabilities of a lume?"

Lumes are a relatively primitive technology. The Adi Shakti can connect with any earthly information system.

"This is awesome!"

Ra laughs and soon the Sikh joins in the mirth. I feel like the new kid on the block.

A word of warning. When you first embrace advanced technology it can encourage feelings of arrogance, superiority and power. If you have suppressed anger or buried trauma, these may soon want free rein. There is nothing more important than developing good character and spiritual maturity. If not, you'll go the way of the dark ones. Do you understand?

Grave words. I nod.

Baset and I will be away for a while investigating the Dark Lizard. I advise you to destroy your lume and only use the Adi Shakti. You are in the capable hands of the Sikh. Learn well.

And then he is gone. I immediately feel disoriented. Shifting reality so quickly and completely is hard. What do you hold on to? Where's the secure base?

* * *

Unbelievably, an entire year goes by. I have not seen Ra or Baset and there are moments when I question if they even existed. The Sikh has been more than generous with his spiritual mentorship. I have also enjoyed learning about the politics, economics and culture of India.

I realise now that the focus of the Sikh's teachings has been on developing good character. According to Sikhism the five cardinal vices are lust, anger, greed, pride and worldly attachment. Devotees are expected to be socially responsible and demonstrate this through acts of charity and service. Honest labour is highly valued. Needless to say, I have spent countless hours cleaning the temple floors and working in the community kitchen.

Sikhism rejects all discrimination by caste, creed, race or gender; instead it embraces the idea that all humans are equal. It cherishes truth, acceptance, contentment and contemplation. The Sikh has kindly embossed this teaching on an old piece of wood which hangs in my bedroom: 'Realisation of Truth is higher than all else. Higher still is Truthful Living.'

I remember Ra's words about spiritual maturity, not just as they applied to me but also how they applied to ancient cultures. It is a valuable lesson.

These last twelve months have manifested far more than my spiritual evolution. Since the establishment of the World Peace Organisation there has been a relentless and unprecedented plague of natural disasters across the globe, with a resultant loss of 25% of the human race. It is still hard to come to terms with this reality. Grief pervades every country. Everyone is still trying to adapt.

* * *

I am sitting by a gushing river, deep in my meditation practice, when a crystal clear voice penetrates the silence.

Adam, this is Ra!

It is startling on so many levels. "Ra? Is that really you? I thought you had left the planet or something."

It's been a busy year. Good that you were ensconced in India. How are your studies coming along?

Mixed feelings. I want to swear at him for abandoning me here, for the sudden change in my circumstances, for losing the job I love. However, I am grateful for the spiritual opportunity and the moments of wonderful peace. I am also reminded of the current plight of the planet and the possibility that Ra's mission may actually be real.

I bite my tongue. "The Sikh has taken good care of me. I have learned a lot."

Are you ready to move to the next level?

"Does this mean moving to another country?"

We need you to find the Star Child. He is difficult to locate but Baset senses that he is living near Mount Kailash.

"Mount Kailash across the Indo-China border? What am I supposed to do when I find him?"

Just be with him. He is part of the overall plan. Keep searching for the sacred objects.

"Am I ever going to see you again?"

Of course, but for now my presence will only endanger you. You are safer away from me.

"Ah, I see."

Ask the Star Child about the Diamond Thunderbolt. Tell him it's time. Enjoy your journey!

It all goes quiet. I close my eyes. Where is my still centre? I am not brilliant at all this adaptation. I prefer a more structured life and a sense of control. Is that naive? Is control possible in a world of constant change? Maybe I need to embrace the concepts of surrender and flow.

I give up the meditation and go find Sikh Nanak. Perhaps he will have some advice.

He is in the community kitchen and comes bounding over immediately, effusive and smiling as always. "You heard from Ra?" I nod. "Are you going to be travelling somewhere?"

"Mount Kailash, apparently."

"A difficult journey. The Indian border is a day's drive from here. I can drop you in Moorang. It will be my honour to take you."

"That's incredibly generous of you. I could not possibly accept."

"No, no, I insist. That's settled then. I am free tomorrow. Will that suit?"

Surrender and flow, surrender and flow. "Thank you. I will sort my things. Probably best to take my backpack and leave the suitcase here."

"Yes, I agree. How do you feel about a small celebratory dinner with close friends tonight?"

"Sounds wonderful. Thank you again."

The evening is spent enjoying delicious vegetarian food and receiving copious farewell blessings. These are truly spiritual people – bright and beautiful lights shining on our planet. I express my indebtedness and deep gratitude for the time I have spent here.

* * *

Moorang is pretty desolate with few people to be seen. The Sikh has organised a Tibetan guide to show me around. We locate him at the Caandi Cafe where we relish a dinner of hot spicy noodles, vegetables and chai. Finally the Sikh departs with an affectionate smile: "God bless you, my friend." I return a bow: "Sat Sri Akal!"

The next morning we take a walk through the hills. The guide points out the formidable Himalaya Mountains, explaining that this extensive 'abode of snow' crosses Pakistan, India, China, Nepal and Bhutan. It is the highest mountain range in the world and includes the famous peaks of Everest and K2, as well as other peaks that are sacred to the Hindus, Buddhists and Sikhs.

Mount Kailash is located in the Tibetan Autonomous Region of China, formerly known as western Tibet.

"Respectfully, it would have been easier to fly to Kathmandu in Nepal and travel from there. But you are paying me well so we will be driving. This will take many days over rough roads. How are you with altitude? Are you fit and healthy?"

I answer all his questions and we spend the next few days crossing difficult terrain, sleeping in expedition tents and enjoying the spectacular scenery. When Mount Kailash finally comes into view, it is breathtaking: A great mass of black rock with a symmetrical snow-covered peak rising to 6,714 metres, situated in one of the most rugged parts of the Himalayas.

According to my guide this is a supremely sacred site to four religions: Hindus, Buddhists, Jains and followers of the indigenous Tibetan religion of Bön. These faiths believe that one of their gods resides at the summit and for thousands of years devotees have been making pilgrimages to circumambulate Mount Kailash.

Myth has it that one trip around the sacred mountain will absolve the sins of a current lifetime; 108 revolutions will absolve the sins of all lifetimes and result in freedom from reincarnation. A similar liberation is attained from one circumambulation of the mountain followed by a plunge in the frigid waters of Lake Manasarovar which lies at an altitude of 4,560 metres.

Interesting. I recall the pilgrims washing in the sacred Amrit Sarovar at the Golden Temple in Punjab. They also performed many circumambulations before entering the Divine Temple. Is there some sacred symbolism here? What does it mean?

The guide is very quick to point out that no pilgrims climb Mount Kailash; all four religions believe it would be a serious act of sacrilege to set foot on its slopes. In fact this action is quite likely to result in death. To ensure I get the point, he reminds me of the notoriously treacherous weather and freezing conditions on the mountain.

After some discussion he agrees to walk around the mountain with me. This arduous task, known as Kora or Parikrama, will take about three days. We drive to the town of Darchen, close to the starting point of the 53-kilometre trek. Once the supplies and backpacks are checked we turn in for the night. Tomorrow is going to be a long day.

My guide is a Buddhist so we circumambulate in a clockwise direction. There are dozens of pilgrims along the way, some slowly prostrating as part of their devotion, others powering along at great speed. It is a challenging but wonderful experience, a time for reflection and contemplation. As we approach the end of day three, I decide to gently ask a few questions.

"Do you believe that there is a god at the summit?"

He pauses, seemingly taken aback. Did I say the wrong thing? Should I have started with a subtler question?

"Buddhists do not believe in God, as in the idea of some almighty omnipotent being. However, according to Buddhist cosmology there are beings existing in higher realms. We call these beings devas or gods. They are powerful but have flaws and imperfections just like humans."

"So where are these gods located?"

He is speaking softly now, his words coming slow. "The gods live in the heavens … it is all myth and mystery anyway … nobody actually sees them nowadays."

"What heavens?"

He stops walking and waves his hands all around. "Everywhere. The heavens are merely different dimensions. The gods exist everywhere."

"I see." Why is he being so cagey? Is he afraid of something? I put my hand on his shoulder and smile: "I welcome your truth. I will not judge what you say."

His face relaxes a little, a sigh escapes his lips. Gazing up at the mountain, he whispers "When I was young and brave I tried to walk to Lake Manasarovar to complete the ritual. It was very tough and I was making good progress …"

"Uh huh." I nod encouragingly.

"There was this man, a Tibetan, dressed like a monk in a saffron-colour robe. He stopped me on the path and asked me where I was going. When I told him, he challenged me, questioning my spiritual character. I was soon filled with doubt and fear."

"And then ..."

"He looked deep in my eyes and said 'To walk the true path, know that you are the sky. All these clouds are just passing by.' I could not understand these words. He told me I would return to this path in the future, bringing something valuable."

"Ok ..."

"Then he disappeared right in front of me. I was so scared that I ran back down the mountain."

"He disappeared?"

"Yes, just like smoke from a fire."

"Is that it? Did he say anything else?"

He scratches his head. "Uh ... his name was Śakra ... I looked it up a few years ago. Buddhist cosmology records that he is the ruler of the Trāyastriṃśa Heaven, a heaven that maintains a physical connection with our reality ... although that could be just another myth." Long pause. "I never told anyone about my adventure because we were not allowed on the mountain."

We continue walking as I try to absorb the information. Is this the rambling of an attention-seeking tour guide? Did he actually meet a god? Shall I tell him I have met one?

A sudden idea flashes. "Do you believe that you must return to Lake Manasarovar to complete the ritual?"

"Yes, of course. But what is valuable to a god?"

"Contemplation, compassion and loving-kindness. Everything else is clouds in the sky."

The guide is pondering these words. The moment stretches quietly.

I continue: "Maybe the gods want us to stop walking around in circles, to stop repeating the same futile behaviours, to stop being reborn into many lifetimes … and to climb straight up the mountain. Maybe they are waiting for us."

"Then why are we forbidden to set foot on the slopes?"

"Because there are forces on this earth that seek to control us, to keep us away from Heaven, to hold us back from the Light. Sometimes you have to ignore what you have been told, listen to your heart, and run as fast as you can to reach Home."

Where are these words coming from? I notice that my right hand is gripping the Adi Shakti. "How far is Lake Manasarovar?"

"About 30 kilometres south of here. We can drive today and camp on the shore overnight."

The guide is fired up now. Perhaps there has been a transmission of energy. Perhaps this is the Sikh's Truthful Living in action.

"Perfect." I smile happily. Our circumambulation complete, we amble down the slopes to find the 4x4 and begin the short drive to the lake.

* * *

The morning light gently cascades through the tents. It sounds like the guide is already cooking breakfast. I step outside, yawn and stretch and breathe in the crisp air. The lake is shimmering a magnificent blue. What a place to wake up!

"Do you know that Lake Manasarovar means Lake of Consciousness or Lake of Mind?"

I shake my head.

"This is a sacred place in Hinduism, Buddhism and Jainism. Pilgrims often venture to bathe in those waters. Hungry?"

"Yes ... thank you."

We sit on a blanket and enjoy the meal together. It is an incredible view: An expansive canvas of sapphire water, black and white mountain peaks, and fluffy white clouds billowing in a bright sky. Impossible to fully capture with a lume.

I turn to the guide: "I am going to meditate in about half an hour. You are welcome to join me."

He smiles. "A kind offer. Afterward I would like to complete the holy ritual in the lake."

There is something magical about meditating with an experienced practitioner. We are soon immersed in a serene and blissful atmosphere. An hour disappears.

I watch the guide wander off toward the lake. The water looks freezing and I am pleased to remain behind. The rising sun is softly warming my face. There is a sudden strong breeze, the scent of jasmine, a sparkling ray of yellow ... and he is standing next to me. I feel the hairs on my arms and neck standing up. Not a word. Not a sound. I keep looking forward. The energy is powerful, godly and humanlike.

His voice is steady and calm. *What are you doing here?*

"I am looking for the Star Child."

Who sent you?

"Ra has returned. He told me to find you. My name is Adam Kadmon."

He moves to the front, holding me with a penetrating gaze. *Adam. A pure soul. I see you have an adventure ahead of you. I wonder if you will survive.*

"The sun-god mentioned the Diamond Thunderbolt."

He points to the lake. *It's in there. I suggest you activate the Adi Shakti.*

I activate the energy shield and walk to the water's edge. The circumference of this lake is 88 kilometres. Where do I start? It could be anywhere. I wade in and notice no change in temperature. That's a relief. I could be here a long time.

After two hours of trawling I feel a sense of despair. I wonder if this is some sort of test, similar to what the guide experienced all those years ago. Come on, think. The Adi Shakti is also a communicate device … it interfaces with Ra's Staff of Light … so perhaps these sacred objects are all connected.

I touch the centre sword and call out: "Diamond Thunderbolt." There is a brief glow underwater. I increase my speed and call out again. It takes about 45 minutes to locate an almost invisible device that grips perfectly in my hand. On either side of the transparent bar is a spindle comprising eight spokes. It is light and easy to carry.

I stumble out the water and present it to the monk. *It is yours to keep, Adam.*

The 4x4 is missing. "What happened to the guide?"

His work is done. I gave him a blessing and sent him on his way.

Surrender and flow, surrender and flow.

A familiar fear touches my stomach. Something is wrong. Dark figures in the distance.

Reconnaissance. You need to destroy them before they send a message.

"What – how?"

Twist one of the spindles. Just one for now, until you learn to control it. Aim, then squeeze the bar.

I quickly turn a spindle and hold it at shoulder height. The dark ones are moving rapidly toward us. An incoming light beam deflects off my shield. Emboldened, I aim and tighten my grip. A blue-white beam fires into the nearby rock. A few more misses then a strange scchhh! sound as a dark being is obliterated.

My heart is leaping in my chest, my mouth is desert-dry. I am in a war zone with no training. The monk is standing calmly with his hands clasped behind his back. Everything is moving in slow motion. I feel strangely detached, firing and firing until the second dark being is annihilated.

I think you will live to see another day. Close the spindle now.

I twist the spokes and wipe my forehead.

My name is Śakra. It is good to meet you. Follow me.

I grab my water bottle from the ground, take a swig and hurry after the Star Child. He has already begun walking up the steep mountain slope.

"So where does the Diamond Thunderbolt come from?" I ask, panting to maintain the hurried pace.

There were many gods on the earth. Before they left they concealed some of their advanced technology at various sacred sites. Your weapon is called the Vajra. It is made entirely of diamond. By the way, if you squeeze the bar when the spindles are closed it will shrink and become more manageable.

I do this and add it to the necklace. How convenient. The gods think of everything.

Over time, as memories blur, advanced technologies become translated into religious symbols. The Vajra has now become a ritual object and spiritual implement in Vajrayana Buddhism. As has the Bell.

He extracts a bell from his pocket and hands it to me. It is a silver colour, completely flat, and about twenty centimetres long. I inspect it for a few moments. "How do you ring a bell that has no clapper?"

The monk laughs. *Is that a Zen koan? Point the Bell to the sky then arc it toward the ground.*

I carry out the motion but nothing happens. A white goose flies slowly overhead. Maybe I am doing it wrong. I sense movement on my right and turn to see a small rock hurtling toward me. Only it isn't hurtling, more like creeping. I have plenty of time to move out the way.

So what do you think?

"I don't understand. What does it do?"

Hope you're a quick learner, Adam.

He strides away and begins pelting rocks at me. The first one bounces off the energy shield. "Are you crazy?" I ring the bell again. The stones decelerate. A little side-stepping and nothing to worry about. "Ok, ok, I get the message."

The Bell slows everything except the Bell-ringer. It gives you a time advantage of thirty seconds.

"These sacred relics are amazing."

Śakra looks me squarely in the eyes. *You do realise there is no turning back?*

I stare at the ground for a moment. "Yes, I do."

What do you believe is most needed now?

"Firmness of spirit and focus for the mission."

Excellent. Let's add the Bell to your necklace.

He shows me how to shrink the sacred object. Thank goodness the devices are so light and portable. I was beginning to wonder if I'd need a neck like a sumo wrestler.

I think back to the Sikh and his generous mentorship. My words and actions are largely due to his teachings. I am starting to appreciate the value of good spiritual character.

"Where to from here?"

We are going to the summit.

* * *

The summit is majestic and awe-inspiring. Śakra leads us into a cave which gradually widens to reveal a vast and magnificent dwelling teeming with beautiful birds and lush vegetation. Pastel shades glimmer across the immense walls. A warm breeze caresses my weary body. The energy is serene and otherworldly.

I sit on a bench hewn from the rock. A fig tree hangs over me. "Is this the home of the gods?"

Indeed. There are sacred places hidden all over this planet. Some gods preferred the high mountains, others the expansive deserts, still others the ocean vistas.

"How long are we going to be here?"

It depends. There is a time for stillness, a time for strategizing and a time for action. Wisdom is knowing when each of these should be applied.

Ok then. I sigh softly.

You hungry?

"Starving."

The trees are laden with fruit; there are seeds and nuts everywhere. The water flowing in that stream is pure. Try to eat slowly as the food is highly nutritious and will satisfy you very quickly.

"Is it organic? I only eat organic."

You have kept your sense of humour. That's good, you're going to need it.

My foraging soon unearths exquisite aromas and delectable surprises, many of which I do not recognise. Blue and white butterflies dance delicately around me and birdsong fills the air. I wonder why the rest of the planet is so different to this paradise.

I return smiling, my hunger comfortably assuaged. The monk is nowhere to be seen. I lay down on the rock bench and close my eyes.

When I awaken, the monk is standing in front of me. *You do know that you are sleeping under the Sacred Fig? This Bodhi is the very tree under which the Buddha became enlightened.*

"Really?" I shrug my shoulders. "I don't feel any different." Śakra dissolves into laughter and a shiny amulet bursts from his robe.

I stare at the polished stone. It looks like obsidian with some type of reflective covering. "Are you going to tell me what that is?"

He removes it from his neck and hands it to me. *It is one of the sacred objects. Part of my mission.*

Elongated, cylindrical, with a glassy black texture. Yep, it's obsidian. Formed when volcanic lava comes into contact with water, forcing it to cool so quickly that it cannot crystallise.

"May I?" He nods. I extract the stone from the silver sheath and inspect the strange etching.

That's a yantra – a mystical or astronomical diagram. It magically holds the essence of a concept or an idea.

I run my fingers along the intricate diagram. It looks like a cross with each end curling slightly to the left. "What does it mean?"

It is the symbol of Divine Tantra, the merging of Shiva and Shakti. The long vertical line refers to the deeper esoteric elements of Tantra while the shorter horizontal line alludes to the earthly aspects.

"No idea what you're talking about."

He gets up, beckoning me to follow. Carved into the nearby wall is a series of ornate pictographs. The story begins with the portrayal of a divine male and female.

Shiva and Shakti were gods who brought Tantra to the earth. This was their home. Along with many other gods they spread the message of loving-kindness and responsibility, but they focused their teachings on romantic love, surrender and union.

One day a courageous priest made the forbidden climb to the summit of Mount Kailash. The Tantra gods had been waiting for an individual with whom they could share their deepest and most sacred teachings. They subjected him to the Impeccability Test reserved for divine apprentices. He passed and spent many years learning in this paradise.

Upon graduation the priest was directed to preserve and protect the divine knowledge. Shiva entrusted him with the Tantra Stone, a lingam-shaped obsidian stone set in a yoni-shaped silver sheath. This celestial object symbolises the perfect balance of the Divine Masculine and Divine Feminine, an equilibrium that maintains optimal growth, progress and peace on earth.

Due to the heavenly and earthly wars the Tantra Stone fragmented into seven pieces and was scattered throughout the planet. The masculine-feminine balance was broken, resulting in a long history of patriarchy, misogyny, female subjugation, pollution and environmental devastation, followed by the rise of feminism and equality movements, culminating in the modern dilemma of disoriented apologetic males and angry faux feminists. Many cultures are still stuck in the early or middle parts of this cycle.

"Wow. That's a lot to absorb."

Wait, it gets better. By 2014 the relentless and dedicated priest had collected five of the missing pieces from hidden vaults and sacred sites around the planet. There was a simultaneous rise in tantric teachings throughout the earth. Unfortunately the Tantra Stone is only fully activated when all seven stones are reunited and sheathed in the silver yoni.

"There are still two pieces missing? I can't see the breaks."

That's because the stones meld seamlessly together.

When I look up, Śakra is pointing to the last pictograph.

"Is that the end of the story?"

What do you think?

"Um, well ... how did you come to possess the Tantra Stone?"

The monk is standing there, staring at me.

"Ah ... it's a true story ... oh, wait ... you are the priest?" He nods. "Of course ... the Star Child, apprentice to the gods."

He is still looking expectantly at me. "Ok ... you have a global mission as a Watcher ... you seek the last two stones as part of your mission ... this is why I am joining you ... and I am probably an apprentice too and don't even know it. The story on the wall is magically writing itself as our adventure unfolds."

Śakra pats me on the back. *You had me a little worried but I think you're going to make it.*

He takes the Tantra Stone and places it on his necklace.

"I gather that's the small version?"

Yes. The missing stones are at least the size of a football. The yantra lights up in the vicinity of the missing pieces, usually within a five kilometre radius.

"That sounds helpful."

Everything we have discussed refers to the horizontal aspect of Tantra. This pragmatic earthly knowledge has spread to teachers far and wide across the planet. The vertical aspect of Tantra is deep and esoteric and we will explore this at a later stage. Your lesson is finished.

A huge stretch overwhelms my body. I need to gather a couple of delicious nibbles, return to the bench under the Bodhi tree and digest all these teachings. Then find somewhere soft to sleep. It's been quite a long day.

* * *

I wake up ensconced in a huge leaf just a metre off the ground. No memory of falling asleep but feel marvellous and refreshed. It's been like this for weeks.

I call out to Śakra but hear only resounding silence.

Somehow I have managed to hold onto my beloved solitude. I truly appreciate moments like this – left alone in my own company. Perhaps I am a little different to most people. I have never had a romantic relationship, nor do I desire one. I sense this calling in the background, something that encourages me to be alone, that makes me feel like I am waiting … waiting …

You are not alone, Adam.

I jump. "How did you do that? Were you once a ninja?"

He smiles. *There are others like you. Many advanced souls have incarnated to support this challenging seven-year period. Their lights will truly begin to shine during the second 42-month cycle. They too have this sense of waiting.*

"Why, what's it all about?"

Light versus dark. Good versus evil. An age-old struggle across many realities.

"Terrible atrocities have been committed all over this earth. We have a history of suffering, violence and war. But aren't these just bad decisions on our part? Is it really evil?"

The light and the dark pervade your planet. But every being has a supreme gift – free will. You can live as you choose and align yourself as you see fit. However, the nature of darkness is destruction and disconnection. It takes you further and further from the Source until the agony becomes excruciating. And it's a long road back.

"So the dark ones are in pain?"

Pain, fear, anxiety, confusion. They desperately attack any light they encounter because they believe that it will obliterate them.

"And will it?"

Of course, that's the whole point.

"Why don't they just sit in the corner and leave the rest of us alone?"

You know the saying 'misery loves company'? Dark ones try to entice souls down to their level. If you could see their fury and agony you would run away and avoid them. So they usually pose as harmless strangers or disgruntled friends and attempt to draw you in through a sense of camaraderie. Sometimes they just whisper in your ear. 'Hey, let's moan together ... let's share our negativity and bitterness ... hmm, how about a step further ... let's knock someone who does good ... let's write comments that disparage a light worker ... throw in a few untruths ... why should anyone be happy if I am not happy? ... let's bite and criticise those who work for the good of the planet ... in what way can we disrupt the peace of those who do what they love? ... ok, let's step it up ... how can we harm those who live in service to the Light? ... oh, here's another idea ... you ready for a little aggression?'

"Isn't that just human nature?"

No! It's free will. It's the choices you make every day. The dark road is endless. Once you set foot on it, where will you stop?

"That's a bit scary."

Is it? Not for people who choose to live with spiritual maturity. Do you think it is just a matter of ethics and morals?

"Obviously not ..."

The gods of light, the precursors of the great religions, the great spiritual teachers – they all taught the same things: loving-kindness, compassion, forgiveness, acceptance, equality, respect, responsibility, gratitude and service. Why?

"To put us on the path of light."

Exactly!

"To help us avoid the temptation of darkness."

Precisely.

"To guide us to return to the Source."

Indeed.

"So all those religious myths of heaven and hell ... those are not places outside of us, they are states of being ... Hell is what you generate when you walk the path of darkness ... Heaven is what you manifest as you walk the path of light ..."

The question is: What kind of reality do you want to create?

"I choose ... to live authentically and ignore the lure of half-truths and untruths ... to walk away from complaining, negativity and bitterness ... to behave with courage, compassion and forgiveness ... to do no harm and accept no harm."

As you now clearly understand, spiritual maturity is important on many levels.

I nod. "It has prepared me for my journey into the sacred knowledge."

Have you checked the newsfeed?

I activate the Adi Shakti and watch the hologram.

'Fifteen months have passed since the establishment of the World Peace Organisation. The eccentric politician, founder and leader of this organisation has been working tirelessly to ensure that the WPO delivers on its promises. Apophis has managed to convince world leaders and the super-wealthy to invest in a spate of new technologies designed to eradicate hunger and help the poor. Already these technologies are feeding and empowering people throughout the Middle East, Europe and Africa and creating conditions for future economic independence. Over the coming months Apophis plans to hold talks to discuss ways to increase peace and unity on these continents.'

"That's impressive."

Behold the masterful seduction strategy and smoky mirrors of the Dark Lizard!

I am sure these gods attend drama classes. Excusing myself, I amble over to the shade of the Bodhi tree. There is much to ponder and this is my favourite spot for silent contemplation.

* * *

Presumably Ra and Baset are seeing some action because it's pretty quiet here at the Śakra cave. The monk disappears at odd times so something must be happening. Admittedly some of his lectures are quite deep and often require long periods of reflection, but I can't believe another six months have gone by.

Apophis' popularity and trust among the peoples of the world are increasing. Trying to destroy him now would probably send the wrong message. Unfortunately every month that passes in the current 42-month cycle gives him the opportunity to gain more authority and power.

After a long meditation I go find Śakra and give voice to my thoughts.

"What are the dark ones doing? They can't just be hunting for us."

They are preparing the way for Apophis' rise to power. Taking the form of humans, they are accessing high levels of political office. They have even infiltrated some religious organisations. Considering the dark hearts of some of your human leaders, this is not very difficult. People are bought, bribed and coerced. Business as usual really.

Is that Śakra's sense of humour?

They are also manoeuvring their technology and ships into strategically optimum positions. This is what Ra, Baset and I are closely monitoring. When the next cycle begins they want to seize power quickly and efficiently. At this stage it's like a game of chess – plenty of watching, planning and patience.

"Why does the Dark Lizard have numerous dark assistants but our side consists of a god, a monk and a cat?"

Yes, but what a cat! Have you seen how she moves?

"Seriously though."

Why do you think?

"Do you always answer a question with a question?"

Do I do that?

"Quite often."

The answer is the same for your previous question.

"Huh?" Oh no, it's the Śakra stare. It means that I need to think.

I rub my chin and watch a hovering butterfly. What did Ra teach me?

"There used to be many gods on earth ... they learned that powerful leaders and priests tend to create disempowered peoples ... Ra is cautiously observing Apophis and deciding on the best strategy ... Creating another war in the heavens may cause humans to become fearful, shocked and disoriented ... or, even worse, dependent ... The gods established many of the world's religions, basing them on the principles of unconditional love and responsibility for self, others and the planet ... Then the gods left and humans were expected to grow up and take charge ... and the same idea still applies."

Hence the policy of minimal interference.

"The reason you ask me questions is so that I learn to think for myself. You are pushing me to become knowledgeable, wise and independent."

My work here is done.

"No, it's not. There is still plenty I need to learn."

He turns away from me, leaps and disappears without warning. I shout at the empty space: "Ok, I didn't know you could that.

Heard about it but didn't know for sure." Instinctively I rip the Bell from the chain and ring it. Close scrutiny reveals a subtle shimmering circle. I dip my hand and it vanishes. I hesitate then jump. Blue light streaks past on all sides.

I fall onto the desert sand. Śakra is walking a few metres ahead. He halts and shouts over his shoulder. *You are going to have to work on your landing.*

Scrambling to get up, I badger him with questions. "What happened? Where are we? How did you do that?"

He leans forward and pulls out a chain covered in sacred ornaments. *Now this, Adam, is a necklace!*

* * *

We are trundling through the sand and I am struggling to keep up.

"Was that some sort of space-time portal?"

Indeed. Only for use in earth reality.

"How long does the window remain open?"

Five seconds. You made it because you rang the Bell.

"How many times can you use it?"

As often as you like.

"Did you activate it via a sacred object?"

Of course.

"Awesome."

What's the downside?

"Um … it's energy … it has a particular energy signature …"

A dark ship looms on the horizon.

"Oh no."

Oh yes.

"I guess that necklace makes you a valuable target."

And you.

I swallow hard.

Stand still and do not activate any objects.

We wait and wait. My mouth becomes parched.

Śakra is staring intently ahead. Now there are three ships.

Activate everything!

The last altercation gave me great motivation to master the weapon. It takes mere seconds to pop the energy shield and twist both spindles of the Vajra.

Just remember that there are two ends to that device.

I nod and force a smile.

Śakra removes a golden bird from his chain.

Then all hell breaks loose.

Thirsty, light-headed, one ship directly ahead, others taking each flank, moving so fast, beams blasting everywhere, taking hits to the shield, stunned, golden bird flung into the air, a screech of red feathers and talons assaulting the front ship, dark ones on all sides, firing, firing, ship exploding in a shock of light … then the pause, everyone feels it … a strange quiet space … breathing slows … field of vision widens … clarity … calm … both ships turning in unison, lining up the monk … too many dark ones distracting him … firing huge beams …

I ring the Bell.

"Śakra!" My scream echoes oddly … running … reach him in seconds … push him to the ground … fire a circular arc at the dark ones … line up the ships along each spindle and squeeze like crazy … another shock of light … a terrible whump hits me … blackness …

Adam!

I hear the monk calling me in the distance.

Adam!

He sounds far away.

Adam, wake up.

I am shaking all over. "Where's the Vajra?"

It's ok, we defeated them. I turned it off.

He hands me a flask of water. I gulp wildly.

We sit for a while and let my senses return. My body is still pumping with adrenaline. It's hard to stay still. It takes some time before I begin to relax.

You saved my life.

"You don't have a shield?"

The sacred objects are not duplicated. There is only one shield.

"Oh."

You may not be a soldier but you are a quick thinker and a pure soul.

"You would have done the same for me."

Indeed.

"What was your sacred object?"

The Phoenix – the flaming bird.

"Yes, and …?"

It is an enormous fire-breathing bird with vicious talons. Reduces airships to ashes. Regenerates if destroyed.

"Was it destroyed?"

Yes, in the blast from the first ship. It's now back on the necklace. Can't use it for the next seven days.

"Amazing."

We all live to fight another day.

"Are you going to tell me why we are here? Where are we anyway?"

Saudi Arabia, the largest country in the Middle East. I finally guessed the location of the sixth stone.

"Only now?"

I've been turning over lots of sacred stones. Hope this one is the real deal.

I look around. "Do you know that Saudi Arabia is 95% desert? It includes the Rub' Al Khali, the biggest mass of sand on the planet."

Are you trying to ask me a question?

"It's scorching out here! Are we going to walk?"

You've been in paradise too long. We need to keep a low profile. We are in the stronghold of Apophis.

"Where are we exactly?"

Just east of Medina, one of Islam's holiest cities. We are going to meet an imam there.

"An imam?"

A scholar, community leader and religious teacher. A man named Abu Talib.

"A member of the Council of Light?"

Of course.

"Why are we meeting him?"

He's going to escort us to Mecca.

"Please tell me the sixth stone is not in Islam's holiest city."

Śakra looks at me and smiles. *I think the sixth stone is in Mecca.*

I cast my eyes upward and sigh heavily.

* * *

"As-Salamu Alaykum!" Abu Talib greets us reverently.

Peace be upon you!

I follow the protocol and receive a warm embrace from Abu.

"And who is your good friend?"

This is Adam, the spiritual leader of the future.

He bows deferentially. "An honour to meet you."

My cheeks flush slightly. "Don't listen to him. It's just his sense of humour."

The imam conveys a caution. "Keep your sacred objects inactive. These are difficult times."

Can you hide us safely?

"Yes, yes, no problem."

Abu leads us to a secure house where he organises dinner. Great timing. Once the body settles, these skirmishes leave you pretty hungry. When the food arrives I am pleasantly surprised to see meat and bread. It's a nice change from the many months of vegetarian living.

Śakra refuses to eat anything. No one says a word about it.

According to the imam, Medina means 'radiant city'. It is the second holiest city in Islam after Mecca and the burial place of the Islamic Prophet Muhammad. Most of the city is off limits to non-Muslims.

Abu indicates with his hand. "You will need to wear these. And I suggest you let your beard grow."

There is an immediate sense of diminishing freedom. I shift uncomfortably on my chair. Why all these rules? The Golden Temple at Punjab welcomed anyone irrespective of religion, creed or gender. Surely the point of all religion is to lead people deeper into liberty, equality, acceptance and respect?

I am irked. I start thinking about the condition of our world. How is it that dictatorships, poverty, violence and war still exist? No one in their heart of hearts wants these to continue. Power and wealth are concentrated in the hands of a minority who for the most part selfishly pursue their own interests. The middle class are complacent – checkmated by a combination of comfortable living and debt. If they had less, they might rise up and use their self-subjugated power. The poor are just desperately trying to survive.

Politics, economics and religion are a formidable triad that controls the people of this planet.

The monk puts his hand on my shoulder. My mind becomes filled with a vision: Women and children marching in streets across the world ... protesting ... colourful banners saying 'No More!' ... 'This Ends Now!" ... Men of all races, cultures and creeds forced to look at their own action and inaction ... watching their loved ones demanding change ... insisting on a new way.

Śakra breaks the reverie. *We will destroy the dark lattice together.*

I nod quietly. He gets up and walks outside.

The imam moves closer to me. "Don't worry about the Star Child. He is melancholic. It is only the Red Sea separating Medina from Ethiopia. He grieves for the Guardian of the Earth. She was the epitome of grace, dance, passion, joy and fierce protectiveness. She was as quiet and powerful as Nature itself."

"I didn't know the gods could feel sad."

He looks thoughtfully at the ground. "Why do people put masters and gods on pedestals? The Council of Light comprises religious leaders, spiritual teachers, enlightened masters and even a mystical author. We have all been initiated into the Mystery. We have all entered the Light. But we are still human beings in limited bodies, subject to the forces of gravity and ageing; we still have minds and hearts, subject to the occasional misguided thought or intense emotion.

"The gods may have higher-level bodies and advanced technology, but they are no different to us. You cannot escape the full experience of Life unless you return to the Source."

I laugh. "So no one's perfect."

"Exactly. This is why all the great teachers have spread the same ideas: acceptance, tolerance, compassion, forgiveness, loving-kindness. There is no need for religion. There is only the Source and the multi-dimensions."

"This message of spiritual maturity keeps coming up."

Abu strokes his beard for a few moments. "Each one of us chooses how to conduct ourselves on this planet. Every word and every action move us closer to or further from the Source. Poor choices only prolong one's own suffering."

I brush a few crumbs from the table. "All the answers are laying open before us."

"Absolutely. If you look deeply, you will find everything. Over the centuries spiritual teachings have been corrupted, religious books rewritten and sacred artefacts hidden, but embedded within every holy object is the Truth."

"You sound like a heretic. Careful you don't get burned at the stake."

The imam smiles. "My first allegiance is to Light, Love and Truth."

With those wonderful words ringing in my ears, I wander off to brush my teeth and rest my weary head. I am looking forward to some serious sleep.

* * *

In the morning Śakra is gone. I feel abandoned in a strange country again. To be fair, I have never been without a guardian, nutritious food and a warm bed, but I miss a place called home.

I excuse myself after breakfast and find a quiet place to meditate. Regular meditation produces a calmness in me, clearer thinking and wonderful moments of no-mind. It allows me to experience that peaceful still centre residing within each one of us.

Over the next few days the imam takes the opportunity to share more of his religious beliefs and spiritual understanding. He explains that true Islam is about doing good deeds to all living beings while opposing injustice and evil. Like many religions it has been misinterpreted and manipulated to serve political interests.

He sighs hopefully. "I believe that one day all religions will rediscover the Truth upon which they were founded: Light, Love, Compassion and Responsibility. It's that simple."

After six weeks Śakra bursts through the door. He looks exhausted, bearing a limp and an ugly laceration across his cheek. Abu assigns immediate medical assistance, a hot bath and a soft bed. The monk does not stir for days.

"A mission of vengeance. I wonder how many dark ones were annihilated."

There goes the pedestal ... I prefer my monks to be serene and imperturbable.

"Have you ever noticed how even the most precious things acquire scratches?"

I nod. Is Abu alluding to the idea of acceptance? Allowing others to be completely who they are and not projecting our desires onto them? What is happening to me? There seems to be a continual shift of knowledge and a deepening wisdom. Am I changing from an adolescent to a spiritual adult? Am I evolving into a butterfly? My wings are probably still wet but I am looking forward to stretching and flying.

Good morning, Adam.

"Hey, how are you? Was your battle worth it?"

Probably wasn't the most sensible strategy. But I have dented the lattice and bought us some time. You'd think an ancient Watcher would have more patience.

"Someone once told me that there is a time for stillness, a time for strategizing and a time for action."

Touché.

"So what's the plan?"

One of the Five Pillars of Islam requires every Muslim to perform the Hajj pilgrimage at least once in his or her lifetime. This involves travelling to Mecca and walking seven times around the Kaaba in a counter-clockwise direction.

"The Kaaba?"

The Kaaba or Noble Cube is a cuboid-shaped building with a mosque built around it, the Masjid al-Haram or Sacred Mosque. It is the most sacred site in Islam and is restricted to Muslim pilgrims. All Muslims around the world face the Kaaba during prayers, no matter where they are.

"How is this related to your mission?"

The Black Stone is the eastern cornerstone of the Kaaba and is revered as a sacred relic. Muslim pilgrims attempt to kiss the Black Stone during their circumambulations.

"This has trouble written all over it."

Abu chimes in: "Myth suggests that it is a divine meteorite sent by God. History records that the prophet Muhammad set the stone into the Kaaba wall in the year 605 AD. The Black Stone is mounted in a silver sheath."

"Are we going to use the space-time portal?"

It's called a Loophole. And, no, we can't afford to create an energy ripple.

"Loophole means 'an ambiguity within a set of rules' – what a perfect name."

Thank you for explaining that to me.

I ignore his grumpiness. Perhaps his body is still hurting. "Are we going to travel by car?"

"Yes. The Hajj takes place in June this year so we are right on time. The crowds will hide us. We will drive from here to Badr then hug the coast until we get to Mecca. It takes about six hours."

"When do we leave?"

Tomorrow morning.

"How did I know you were going to say that?"

I spend the rest of the day feeling apprehensive. It's one thing annoying a monk but I am deeply reluctant to invade a hornets' nest of religious zealots.

* * *

The drive to Mecca is without incident. For all intents and purposes we look like regular pilgrims in our white ihrams and sandals.

Our entry into the Sacred Mosque goes unnoticed. We blend into the heaving throng and begin our circumambulations. My heart is beating in my throat. I am carrying my digging tools under my garment. It will be my job to remove the stone while the other two create a distraction. I hope the monk has a good plan.

As we begin the seventh circuit Abu moves us toward the eastern corner of the Kaaba. Śakra pulls out the Tantra Stone and unsheathes it cautiously. The yantra is lit up. It's a go! My nerves are jangly and every footstep is making me feel spaced-out. There are people everywhere. This does not seem possible.

From the corner of my eye I notice a deft flick of the wrist. Suddenly the sky is filled with an enormous golden bird flapping blood-red wings. Chaos ensues. Pilgrims falling flat on the ground, others shouting boldly, most running in every direction. Abu draws me close and we locate the stone. It is about thirty centimetres in diameter and my experienced hands extract it in minutes. A momentary fumble and the Black Stone falls at my feet. I scoop it up and put it in the sturdy white bag.

Śakra grabs us and we begin a fast walk to the exit. Then the screaming begins. Words I do not understand. Armed guards appear ahead. The removal has been discovered. I activate the Adi Shakti and begin running. I look back for a moment to witness a huge swathe of fire in the sky.

Weaving through the palm trees, surrounded by a mass of devotees, we make it to the parking place. Abu starts the engine and hurriedly tries to escape the crowd. Śakra extracts the Tantra Stone and asks me to hand him the missing piece. There is a brief flash of light as the stones meld seamlessly. A satisfied smile dashes across his face.

We are driving west toward the Red Sea. The Phoenix flies above us for a while then drops out of the sky and lands in the monk's hand. It is promptly inserted onto the necklace along with the Tantra Stone. I deactivate the energy shield. It is very quiet in the car. Not sure if it's mission nerves or the fact that we are holding our collective breath.

About an hour passes and we arrive at Jeddah seaport. Abu directs us to a waiting felucca which has the capacity for about ten passengers. I briefly admire its rig of two lateen sails. The captain smiles warmly and shakes our hands. "Peace be upon you" resounds everywhere.

The boat is heading north along the Red Sea. I ask Śakra about our destination.

We will be sailing through the Gulf of Aqaba to reach the Taba border-crossing into Israel.

"The seventh stone?"

He sighs. *I hope so.*

The sun is still warm so I find a shady spot and settle down to some meditative sea-gazing.

* * *

"So where do we start?"

I have no idea. Let's head to the Old City in Jerusalem.

We hire a 4x4 and I volunteer to drive. Abu gives directions and noting that he has a captive audience, says. "Let me tell you about this interesting and conflicted place."

I nod quietly.

"Within the modern city of Jerusalem is a walled area called the Old City which is divided into the Muslim Quarter, the Christian Quarter, the Jewish Quarter and the Armenian Quarter. The Old City contains sites sacrosanct to these religions."

Sounds challenging already.

"The Old City also contains a natural plateau called the Temple Mount which measures approximately 150,000 square metres. While the Church of the Holy Sepulchre is safely ensconced in the Christian Quarter, the Temple Mount has become a strongly contested religious site for Jews and Muslims."

"Ok, start with the Jewish report."

"In the middle of the Temple Mount is a sacred rock called the Foundation Stone which covers a cavern known as the Well of Souls. The Stone also stands directly over the buried remains of the Holy of Holies of the Temple of Solomon, the place where the High Priest communicated directly with God. This area is regarded as the spiritual junction of heaven and earth, and the resting place of the Divine Presence. Understandably, it is the holiest site in Judaism and Jews traditionally face it while praying."

Śakra is paying close attention now.

"What about the Muslim account?"

"After the Muslim conquest of Jerusalem in 637 AD, construction of the al-Aqsa Mosque and the Dome of the Rock began on the Temple Mount. The al-Aqsa Mosque was built on the one end of the Temple Mount and the Dome of the Rock was built directly over the Foundation Stone."

I shake my head. "Why on earth did they do that?"

"The stone is also considered sacred in Islam. The Prophet Muhammad is believed to have made a mystical Night Journey from Mecca to the Temple Mount, then ascended to heaven to talk with God. The stone marks the place of ascension. The Dome of the Rock is a Muslim shrine. The entire Temple Mount, also known as al-Haram ash-Sharif or Noble Sanctuary, is considered the third holiest site in Islam, after the Kaaba in Mecca and the Mosque of the Prophet in Medina."

Abu, set our course for the Temple Mount.

I groan inwardly. Surely not the Foundation Stone? It's just a rock under a shrine.

Abu steers me in another direction. "You haven't asked about the Christians."

"Tell me about the Christians."

"The Church of the Holy Sepulchre, also called the Basilica of the Holy Sepulchre, is located in the Christian Quarter of the Old City. The site is venerated as the location of the crucifixion of Jesus, at Golgotha or the Hill of Calvary, as well as the place of his burial and resurrection, the Sepulchre. Consequently this church is a very important pilgrimage destination for Christians."

I blink a few times.

"Wait a minute. Three major religions all having a similar story of ascension and direct communication with God?"

Thought you'd never ask.

"What's the connection?"

Truth is lost in the mists of time and replaced by holy sites and sacred buildings.

"What are you talking about?"

Someone ascends and remembers that they are God. They return overflowing with Light and Love. However, words have abandoned them. Devotees and strangers sense the divine energy and try to formulate a coherent set of teachings. Excited by this Presence, they spread the Word. They must convince others to follow the New Way. But the further they travel from the Master, the less the Presence is felt. So they form rules and rituals and practices to harness and capture the divine energy. Eventually the Master leaves, as all Masters do, and followers are left empty and abandoned. In desperation they form a religion. A religion often subsequently bent and manipulated for political and economic control.

I take a deep breath. The monk's words are starting to make sense. Each one of us is responsible for our own journey toward the Light. The goal, if we choose it, is our own ascension and our own awakening. We are the holy city, the sacred stone and the High Priest. We can meet God.

We arrive outside the Temple Mount, park the 4x4 and find a place to eat. After some time we make our way to the Dome of the Rock, a beautiful shrine covered in colourful Iznik tiles with a distinctive golden dome on the roof. The doorway is guarded by eight pillars and opens into a lavish interior comprising plush carpets, stained-glass windows, mosaic, faience, marble and elegant Qur'anic inscriptions.

Śakra gets down to business, quietly extracting the Tantra Stone. I peer over his shoulder. Nothing is lit up. What a relief. We are not going to upset any more religious zealots. I feel like doing a little dance. I do my best not to smile.

He looks disappointed. I think about his lifelong mission. "How about under the Dome of the Rock?"

Under?

"I don't know. Maybe the signal is covered by the shrine."

We walk outside where Śakra confers with Abu. I am beginning to wish I hadn't said anything.

It's risky but I am going to use the Loophole. Abu will stay here. You coming?

Before I can speak, he rips a silver circle from the necklace and throws it to the ground. A loophole opens and we jump through.

Dark! Can't see a thing. I knock my head against a rock.

Activate the Adi Shakti.

I do so. To my surprise, everything lights up. "Didn't know it could do that. Where are we?"

The Well of Souls. We must be quick; we have activated three sacred objects.

He checks the yantra again but only dark obsidian shines back at him.

I felt sure we would find the missing piece.

"What are these symbols on the wall?"

They refer to the Knights Templar, the secret order of the Temple of Solomon.

I brush my hand across the indentations ... an archaeologist's dream. Sighing, I flick the encrusted dirt away and uncover the outline of an archway. "Do you think this was originally a door?" I find a sharp stone and scrape the hardened limestone but it seems there is only solid rock ahead. Resting my hand for a moment, my eyes scan the archway. There appears to be a niche in the doorpost. I delicately probe and sweep until the recess is revealed. Reaching in, I extract a small ornate container.

"What do you suppose this is?"

Let me see. Ah, a sacred Mezuzah. These receptacles usually hold a heavenly scripture.

"Never heard of it."

A Mezuzah is God's Word on the Doorpost. It is written about in Kabbalah.

"Kabbalah?"

Kabbalah is a form of Jewish mysticism, a set of esoteric teachings that explains the relationship between the eternal, unchanging and mysterious Ein Sof or No End and the transient universe of creation. Kabbalah began once Adam consumed the fruit of the Tree of Knowledge, revealing the secret of the divine Light and its manifestation in the infinite realities.

Śakra throws down the silver circle and we jump back to the waiting imam.

"What took you so long? We must hurry. Something does not feel right."

It's like walking into another world. The foreboding sense of dark energy. Anomalous body language from a number of passing pilgrims. A strange glance here, a furrowed brow there. We are surrounded by an invisible and ominous militia.

We run to the 4x4. Still no action. Are they watching us or waiting for something?

Drive west to the Port of Ashdod. We don't have much time.

As we race toward the sea Ra's voice bursts into our airspace. *Śakra, what's happening? The grid shows an enormous amount of energy activity in your area.*

We found a Mezuzah. But there is nothing inside; only an etching of a scripture – Ezekiel 1:4-28.

It goes quiet for a while. Then Ra comes on again. *The grid shows eight sacred objects at your location.*

I do a quick calculation. My necklace contains the Adi Shakti, the Vajra and the Bell. The monk's contains at least the Tantra Stone, the Phoenix and the Loophole. "How many have we got?"

Seven.

"The Mezuzah must be a sacred object!"

Are you heading toward the Mediterranean Sea?

"Yes!" I shout.

Get the Mezuzah to the water-goddess. She can bring it to me.

I look at Śakra and shrug my shoulders.

Consider it done.

So … the monk has a sacred object I have not yet seen … there's a mysterious Mezuzah with an unknown function … and there's a water-goddess. Intriguing. Ra has confirmed great energy activity but the dark ones appear to be avoiding a direct confrontation.

"They must be planning a subterfuge … perhaps to capture us alive and obtain our necklaces."

We reach the Port of Ashdod safely. Śakra turns to the imam. *Your journey with us ends here. We are deeply indebted to you. Where do you wish to go?*

"Marrakesh, Morocco. A beautiful oasis of luscious fruit trees and abundant plants, right near the Atlantic Ocean. The perfect place to rest." I give Abu Talib an affectionate hug and slip a rough diamond into his palm. Śakra throws the silver circle to the ground and the words "Peace be with you!" ring through the air. The imam jumps and disappears.

We are walking through the harbour when I ask "How does that sacred object work?"

You simply think of a place you have previously visited and throw the circle.

A serious limitation. "I guess you have travelled extensively."

Indeed.

The monk negotiates passage on a large motorboat. It's amazing what a diamond can organise.

"Where are we going?"

To the island of Crete.

"The water-goddess?"

Hopefully.

"And then what?"

I don't know.

Should I be taking more responsibility? Is there a way I can contribute to this mission?

After a couple of hours of bracing sea air Śakra taps me on the shoulder. *Do you know what day it is?*

I shake my head.

Exactly two years since you met Ra.

Wow, he's right. What a wild ride it has been. I gaze thoughtfully over the calm turquoise sea.

Everything shimmers. Out of nowhere, a dozen black ships on the water, weapons trained on us. "What the –"

Cloaked to be invisible. Waiting for us no doubt.

There's nowhere to run and nowhere to hide. We stare across the waves for a long moment.

Suddenly the captain steps forward and whacks Śakra across the head, knocking him unconscious. Then he shape-shifts into his natural form and stands looking at me. Why is he not doing anything? I raise my hands and try to sense the Adi Shakti. Is it still activated? Is it protecting me?

A movement in the water catches my eye. Long white hair and a silver-blue arm waving furiously. Is that the water-goddess? I react instinctively, grabbing the Mezuzah from the monk's necklace and throwing it hard into the sea. The dark one lunges toward me and connects with the energy shield. We both topple to the deck. I look at him and smile. I know what to do.

I reach for my necklace and ring the Bell. Thirty seconds to act. Find the silver circle, put the monk on my shoulder, think of a place, throw it over the edge of the boat and jump through. We're going to Japan.

* * *

Japan? What are we doing in Japan?

I explain the missing events to the monk.

He smiles. *That's twice you've saved me. You're proving to be a worthwhile apprentice.*

I never know what to make of the Star Child. Is he a god? Is he immortal? No, the other Watcher died. At times he seems so fallible, at times so wise. He has no doubt accrued a vast repository of knowledge and experience during his lengthy stay on earth. I wonder if he feels weary.

It gets a bit lonely.

"Huh?"

To answer your question: I am mortal. Everything that is created is mortal. This is the transient nature of creation. Only the underlying Source lives forever.

"Are you reading my mind?"

Everything is a thought-force. Your beliefs are a bit antiquated so you operate on a limited wavelength. In time this will change.

"What beliefs?"

Do you believe you are just a body? Or a mind? What if you are consciousness? What if you are expressed everywhere and everywhen at the same time? What if there are no past lives but simply one life expressed across multiple dimensions? What if beings in other dimensions are just varying expressions of you?

"Whoa, slow down … you lost me at 'thought-force'…"

You're not ready for the next level?

"What next level?"

He bends down and picks up a few stones. Thrown high in the sky, they gradually fall until they are hovering in a perfect circle above my head. Impressive. Then he leaps into the air, flies through the circle and lands upside down on a single pointed finger.

"The circus is the next level?"

The monk collapses in laughter. After a few minutes he looks around. *It seems we are in the Ryoan-ji Zen Garden in Kyoto. Do you know that this is one of the best stone gardens in Japan?*

I have been waiting for this moment. Placing my hands behind my back, I reply "Indeed."

Śakra smiles. *That word is reserved for fully-fledged monks and graduates of the programme.*

I press on. "Let's start from the top. Japan is an extensive group of islands located in the Pacific Ocean. The name literally means 'sun-origin' which is why it is often called the Land of the Rising

Sun. The four largest islands are Hokkaido, Honshu, Shikoku and Kyushu. Together these make up 97% of Japan's land mass. Honshu, the largest island, is where we find Kyoto, the former capital of Japan, a place exhibiting far more Japanese culture and history than the bright urban jungle of the current capital Tokyo. In Kyoto you can still see women dressed in authentic geisha outfits; men in samurai warrior garb; and traditional Japanese theatre."

I am hungry and tired. It's been a long day.

"The Seven Herb Tofu Restaurant is situated beside the Kyoyochi Pond on the temple grounds. It's along that path."

Soon we are seated on tatami, eating tofu and vegetables, and enjoying the wonderful views. I can see the monk is flagging. "Let's sleep in the temple grounds tonight. The weather has been dry and warm."

After dinner we traipse through a grove of maple and pine and find a soft space hidden among the trees. Within minutes we fall into an exhausted sleep.

* * *

Hope you realise we can't return to the paradise at Mount Kailash. Kyoto is going to be our home for a while.

"I had that feeling ..."

We need a lower profile in order to survive.

"What about the mission?"

In all my years on earth I have learned that life is often a waiting game. One of the secrets to success is patience and preparation. It is about being ready for opportunity when it presents itself.

I sigh. "Ok, how about we visit a few temples?"

Great idea.

We leave Ryoan-ji Temple and walk to Kinkaku-ji Temple which is only a short distance away. The beautiful three-storey building is ensconced in a magnificent strolling garden and perched over a small lake called Mirror Pond. The top two storeys are covered in gold leaf and contain Buddhist relics, giving it the name Temple of the Golden Pavilion. Reminds me of the Dome of the Rock in Jerusalem and the Divine Temple in Punjab. I wonder if gold has a particular spiritual significance.

We travel in an easterly direction for an hour and visit Ginkaku-ji Temple, also known as Temple of the Silver Pavilion. The setting is equally serene, utilising the gorgeous combination of trees and water.

"Time for brunch. I'm starving." The street leading to the temple is host to a few stores selling souvenirs, crafts and food. After a standing meal Śakra mentions a temple located about a kilometre south. Rickshaws are scattered everywhere so we hop on and take an easy journey.

I have been to this temple before. Would you like a briefing?

"Go ahead."

The Kyoto Gozan or 'five great Zen temples of Kyoto' consists of Tenryu-ji, Shokoku-ji, Kennin-ji, Tofuku-ji and Manju-ji. The head temple presiding over the Gozan is Nanzen-ji. This is where we are now headed.

"Sounds impressive."

Nanzen-ji is considered one of the most important Zen Buddhist temples in the world. It comprises twelve sub-temples and several gardens of which only a few are open to the public. Two of the sub-temples also serve vegetarian lunches.

"Is there someone you know at the temple?"

The abbot is a member of the Council of Light.

"That's rather useful."

We arrive at the imposing two-storey gate with its grand pillars. *This is called the Mountain Gate or Dragon Gate. There are stairs to get to the top and the views are magnificent.*

Eventually we make our way down and stroll through the gate to the Hojo or Abbots' Quarters. An elderly man dressed in a long black robe with wide sleeves stands waiting. His face lights up as we approach. "Śakra! How good to see you again."

The Star Child bows deferentially. *Aisatsu!*

"You want to debate with the roshi?"

The monk smiles then looks at me: *The best Rinzai Zen Master of each generation is designated as Abbot of Nanzen-ji.*

I bow humbly.

"You mischievous monk! Strangers and apprentices may need titles and definitions but friends certainly do not. Please call me Koichi."

"My name is Adam."

The abbot leads us to a Zen garden. Positioned against a plain white wall is the typical raked gravel interspersed with rocks, clipped azaleas, maples, pines and moss. Perfectly exquisite.

"One of my favourite places for thinking and meditating: Leaping Tiger Garden."

We bask in the serene energy for a while, then "Are you going to be staying?"

Please. We need a place to lay low. Some clean robes would be wonderful too.

A few words and everything is organised. The bath is sublime and way overdue. I am lying here wondering how I came to lose everything and be dependent on strangers. Something to do with surrender and flow. After some time I dry myself and dress in a fresh robe.

Śakra and I stroll down to the Nanzen-in sub-temple. We meander through the trees and finally settle by the pond garden. The abbot joins us in quiet reflection. The ambience is still and serene and effortless. An hour comfortably trickles away.

"We may as well get your teaching started."

My interest is piqued. I nod.

"Zen is a school of Buddhism that originated in China and spread throughout Vietnam, Korea and Japan. The word Zen can be translated as 'absorption' or 'meditative state'. Zen is less interested in knowledge of sutras and doctrine, rather it focuses on direct insight and understanding through zazen and interaction with a seasoned teacher."

Less theoretical and more experiential. I like it. "What is zazen?"

"Zazen means 'seated meditation'. It is a set of practices that includes developing of one-pointedness of mind, focusing on the present moment, and koan introspection."

It's a way to access the Space Between.

I wonder if all students sound like an echo. "Space Between?"

I met an unusual-looking man a few times. Long white hair and piercing almond-shaped blue eyes. He told me that all of Life is contained in this Moment, in the space between your thoughts, in the pause between your breaths.

Why does that sound so familiar? "You are referring to No-Mind or the Space Between Thoughts?"

Indeed.

Hah! I am finally ahead of the game. Was it a book I read? Let me think.

The abbot swiftly slaps my leg. "It's about being fully present in the moment!"

Śakra laughs out loud. And so my training commences.

* * *

What a privilege to be experiencing Zen. I am wearing the mandatory black robe and starting to feel like a monk. After weeks of breathing exercises I move into present-moment meditations and slowly learn to access the Now. This is rather challenging but the abbot and his stealthy accomplices employ a variety of methods to help my wandering mind.

Autumn is spectacular. I spend hours in joyful contemplation, lost in a storm of orange, yellow and pink leaves. The ground is a blanket of gorgeous colours. A stream gurgles softly in the distance. This is surely the perfect time of year to be ensconced in a Kyoto temple.

And then Spring arrives, encouraging me to reconsider my position. The pink and white cherry blossoms are absolutely breathtaking. With the advent of the new season I graduate to koan work. The abbot explains: "Rinzai Zen emphasises the use of paradoxical puzzles or questions to move you beyond the constraints of mind. It aims to give you direct experience of the Source."

He leaves me to wrestle with this difficult koan: 'Before your parents were born, what is your original face?'

It drives me crazy. I think continually. Moving in circles. Holding it at different angles, in different light. Meditating. Focusing on the Now. My mind stops working. Staring at the trees. Feeling the sun on my back. Then suddenly and slowly ... a series of kenshos ... moments of direct insight into my true nature. I am taken aback. Grasping, I lose it. Chasing, it disappears. Surrendering, it returns.

"You know how to rake?"

"I think so."

"Don't think. Rake."

Raking without thinking ... witnessing the movement of arms ... raking ... listening to the sound of pebbles ... raking ... feeling the breath ... raking ... warmth on skin ... raking ... noticing thought ... raking ... sensing emotion ... raking ... being in the moment ... raking ...

One morning Śakra and the abbot are standing watching me. *The stones are moving.* "No, Adam is moving." I look up and say "Not the stones, not Adam. Mind is moving."

Koichi bows to me. "Satori is not far away."

His words drift in the wind. Raking continues.

Weeks disappear. Time seems to stand still. A single moment stretches into infinity. Adam lives and breathes. I touch a leaf and feel my own hand. It rains and I cry. The sun shines and I understand. Where is the distance between you and me?

Adam, have you seen the newsfeed?

I glance over the abbot's shoulder.

'The past three years have seen Apophis grow in political stature. As leader of the World Peace Organisation he has managed to unite the Middle East and most of Europe and Africa. Countries who belong to the WPO have abundant crops and hunger has been abolished. An unprecedented peace reigns. Who is this man? How is he able to succeed where countless others have failed? Is this the result of altruism? Is this what happens when countries are given advanced technology at minimal cost?

'Even more startling: Despite repeated offers inviting the United States of America to join the WPO, it has steadfastly refused. And today, 7 July 2026, the US has declared the beginning of talks to unite North and South America. There is speculation that a similar peace organisation will be formed. Sources close to the White House have mentioned the presence of shamans and other indigenous consultants, and a cryptic prophecy about the Eagle and the Condor flying together. Stay tuned as we gather more information.'

The abbot comments: "Amazing. What do you think of that, Śakra?"

The monk is studiously watching the hologram as it shifts from Breaking News to a story about a sacred artefact. 'After repeated entreaties from the Anangu people and finally a direct intervention from the Australian government, a British museum is returning a mysterious object to its original home in Australia. We are calling it mysterious because journalists are forbidden to photograph it. Apparently only initiated Anangu males may gaze upon it.'

I can see the Star Child lighting up. Could it be?

Koichi notices the body language too. "You planning to go to Australia?"

We leave for Uluru in an hour.

The abbot scurries off while Śakra disappears into his thoughts. A slight anxiety tickles my stomach. I close my eyes and remember … no attachments … acceptance of reality as it is … surrender.

Koichi returns with a small box and hands it to me. After a deep bow he says "You don't need praise, recognition or accreditation. Your journey is your own. However, here is something you may find useful."

Inside the box, wrapped in soft yellow cloth, is a silver parchment that fits easily in my palm. The calligraphic inscription reads: One Cannot Grasp Water In A Closed Hand.

"It's a Koan for your necklace. You will know what to do with it."

Ah, the famous Zen principles of simplicity and spontaneity.

I bow in gratitude. "Wind blows, leaves scatter."

The Loophole opens. A resounding *Aisatsu!*

* * *

I feel torn between the exciting events, the sense of adventure and my need for a place called home. The spiritual masters teach that home is within and I get glimmers of this during meditation.

However, I long for a place to lay my head ... sunrays filtering through white shutters ... cosy mornings wrapped in a duvet ... a soft touch ... long auburn hair ... blue eyes ... a radiant smile ... such love in her eyes ...

Are you dreaming of a woman?

I snap out of it. "Yes ... no idea why."

Maybe your paths are intersecting. You are starting to sense her energy.

"There's no time for a relationship. We need to focus on the mission."

Spoken like a true warrior. Or a lone ranger.

I ignore the last remark. I haven't been drawn by love. Not yet. And I adore quiet and solitude. What woman would put up with me? I am probably too difficult, too moody, too ...

Adam's in looove, Adam's in looove, Adam's –

"Oh, stop it! Let's find the stone." I look around. "Where have you landed us this time?"

In Australia, mate! The Northern Territory.

"Is that a Spanish accent?"

Śakra laughs. *Perhaps you should add 'sensitive' to your list.*

"What list?"

Sensitive, moody, task-oriented.

"Are you talking about me?"

You can only be yourself. You are the result of so many influences: spiritual, genetic, psychological, social, cultural, political. Best thing to do is fully accept yourself, radiate your inner light and trust that the right partner will gravitate toward you.

"I don't want to be having this conversation … How will I know if she is right for me?"

You will feel it. Most important: If she cannot accept all of you, then she is not the one.

"What do you mean?"

Cultural influences, especially the media and advertising, tell us that we 'deserve' to have a partner with a gorgeous physical body and sparkling personality, full of loving-kindness, with no issues, baggage or hang-ups. We should strive to find this ideal partner and discard anyone who does not meet these criteria.

"Sounds reasonable."

There are so many lonely people in this world. Atomised, isolated and chasing that fantasy. Love is made of real people in real relationships that understand the necessity of compromise and sacrifice. People who know how to communicate their needs but also know how to balance the various needs in a relationship.

"Are you referring to a tantric relationship?"

Let me explain the beauty of Tantra. Imagine you are an unshaped block of marble mounted on a podium. Exposed to the weather for centuries, you gradually become sculpted into a magnificent and unique piece of art. Relationships bring the weather. Love is the sculptor.

Tantra is the journey made by a couple on the way to the Light. It is also the journey made by a family, by communities, by societies, by countries. We each bring our gifts, our talents, our desires, our thoughts, our emotions. We also bring our hurts, our fears, our pain. We learn to truly listen, empathise and accept others as they are. We also learn to strip away our defences and expose our hearts.

"An adventure of the heart?"

Exactly. This life is an Adventure of the Heart. It is not about power and greed and self-serving interests. It is about entanglement in reality – real people, unguarded hearts, deep connections. It's about sharing and visioning and holding hands. It's about vulnerability before each other and surrender before the Mystery. No one can say they know the Truth. No one wants to face death. Yet how many of us ever truly live?

"What has death to do with love?"

To enter into the Light, you have to die. When you truly love, you are gradually burned away until you cease to exist. You become Love. You become the Light. For some this journey takes many lifetimes and many relationships; for others a few intense relationships suffice; a rare few are transformed in one dramatic act.

The journey of Tantra is the wildest exposure of one's own heart and the most loving acceptance of another's heart.

"Why is it so hard to surrender into love?"

Pain and fear. Those dark emotions close hearts and corrupt relationships. Sadly, people are often blind to their own darkness.

"What's the way forward?"

Courage. Forgiveness. Vulnerability. Putting aside hurt and pain and risking it all again.

"Surrendering to the flame of love."

Precisely.

"Hey, we could have eaten lunch before we left."

I was thinking the very same thing.

"Pukulpa pitjama Ananguku ngurakutu." The voice from behind startles me. "Welcome to our Aboriginal Land."

I spin around. "Where did you come from?"

"My name is Mandu." He smiles broadly and shakes my hand.

"Adam. This is Śakra."

"G'day, Śakra. How you doing, my friend?"

A warm embrace and soon they are chatting like long lost companions.

"So, Adam, you know where we are?"

"Australia?"

"You are smack in the middle of the country. Central Australia, in the lowest part of the Northern Territory, home of the Pitjantjatjara people. We prefer to be called Anangu and it's much easier to say." He smiles again. "You guys hungry?"

Starving.

"Come on. Let's get you fed and watered."

It turns out we are located in the Uluru-Kata Tjuta National Park just south of Lake Amadeus. I gaze across the semi-arid landscape of trees, shrubs and wild flowers. The winter sun is warm and pleasant. An immense red rock formation can be seen in the distance.

"You up for bush tucker?"

"Huh?"

"Bush food. Quandong is a type of peach, kutjera is like a raisin. We can make you a kangaroo sandwich too."

"Sounds lovely. Thank you."

During the meal Mandu explains that the park covers 1,320 square kilometres and includes two sacred Aboriginal features – Uluru and Kata Tjuta. The latter is also known as Mount Olga and lies 40 kilometres to the west.

He points to the huge rock formation. "Uluru. English people call it Ayers Rock. That sandstone monolith is 348 metres high and over 9 kilometres in circumference. It was created by our ancestors and contains numerous canyons, waterholes, caves and ancient rock paintings. The Anangu are descendants of the ancestral beings and we take great care of our ancestral land. We do not climb Uluru as it is sacrosanct and we discourage visitors from climbing it."

Another sacred summit that people are forbidden to ascend. How interesting. It seems that nothing has changed on this earth. Kings are now politicians, the money-changers are now stock brokers, and the high priests still control access to the sacred sites. The same people still rule the world. And they say we live in a democracy. What an ingenious charade.

"I wonder when ordinary people will be granted access to the holy places. Why are these gateways to the Light hidden from us?"

Śakra looks at the Aboriginal elder. *Do you want to handle this one?*

He nods. "Peering into the infinite realities brings you closer to understanding your true nature."

"That's a good thing."

"You gradually discover that you are free, that you are a responsible creator, that you no longer need to be constrained within the structure of religion."

"More good news."

"Your awakening destabilises the existing power structure. It threatens the triad of control – the political, economic and religious systems instituted by the puppet-masters."

I rub my chin. "So it is preferred that the masses are kept away from enlightenment."

"Over the centuries religious texts have been rewritten and important teachings removed. Holy artefacts reflecting the truth have been hidden in vaults beyond the public eye. Sacred myths and rituals have been maligned and disparaged. And entry to hallowed sites has been forbidden. All to obfuscate the Light."

Hence our broader mission. The true work of the gods is not to defeat evil but to inspire, educate and encourage the people of this world. It is up to them to take charge. When enough people awaken and then rise up together, their collective light will easily overthrow the dark lattice.

Mandu stands up abruptly. "Take it easy for the rest of the day. Enjoy the scenery. We can visit Uluru in the morning. I have organised accommodation outside the park."

He hands us a map with a couple of encircled areas, then strolls away. I fill my water bottle and tell Śakra that I need to go for a walk and think about everything. Hesitating for a moment, I ask the obvious question: "Is he a member of the Council of Light?"

Of course.

"Aha. See you later."

* * *

We are taking a slow walk to the base of Uluru with plenty of water and a backpack of supplies.

"You do realise that the Anangu own the land of the National Park?"

"Really?"

"Yep. We have leased the land to the Australian government for tourism but we manage the area with the Parks Board. It is imperative that we maintain this land according to the laws of our ancestors. We call this Tjukurpa and it includes our beliefs, laws, culture and history. Anangu land is still inhabited by the spirits of the ancestral creator beings, the Tjukuritja."

"How have you preserved your knowledge?"

"Tjukurpa is recorded by way of carvings, paintings and ritual objects, and is also taught to each generation. The deepest and most sacred teachings are inscribed on holy objects called tjurungas which are only allowed to be handled by initiated males. These are concealed in the inner sanctum."

Where are we headed?

"To an obscure cave on the west side. It is not visible yet."

Has the artefact arrived?

"It was flown in overnight and will be delivered to the cave this morning."

The elders must be quite excited.

I glance at Śakra. I hope he is not going to be disappointed.

We finally arrive at a cave hidden by dense brush. Once inside, a maze of tunnels greets us. I am glad we are being escorted by Mandu as one could easily disappear forever in this labyrinth. Half an hour passes as we walk deeper into the heart of Uluru. Then a huge cavern opens up and a number of elders greet us enthusiastically.

It's a bit surreal.

The monk is conversing in a foreign language. We all share food and there is much conviviality. I retire to a rock bench near a pool of crystal water. Nothing to do but watch and wait. Eventually a runner bursts in, carrying a wooden box. It is given to the chief elder. Śakra wastes no time in extracting the Tantra Stone. The yantra is glowing brightly.

An hour-long ritual takes place which I am not allowed to watch. I close my eyes and doze. There is a lengthy silence then an animated discussion. I surmise the monk is convincing them of the significance of his mission. Sounds like a quarrel. The chief says he needs a few days to think about it. The monk reminds him what is at stake. After much negotiation the stone is surrendered to the Star Child on the proviso that he stays for a few months and shares his knowledge.

The blinding flash seals the deal. We watch in awe as the Tantra Stone completes itself. A mysterious mauve mist fills the cave and streaks of lightning crackle. Even Śakra looks apprehensive. Then an apparition of a curvaceous dark-haired woman appears.

So, monk, you finally fulfilled your duty!

He stands strong; feet apart and hands behind his back. *I have indeed.*

Is this planet ready to unite the masculine and feminine? To rule together with directed wisdom, love, dance, pleasure and poetry? To celebrate everything that each has to offer?

I believe so. It is vital for the next stage.

She seems thoughtful. It all goes quiet.

Is this Adam? The monk nods. *Is he ready?*

He will be.

The energy feels strange. I have the sensation of being scanned, as if she is assessing the qualities of my soul. The Anangu are unmoving and wordless. They have probably never seen a goddess.

I give you both my blessing.

"Shakti?"

She swirls, engaging me with her full force. *Adam?*

"Will I meet the woman in my dream? Is she the one?"

In time. You must follow your destiny.

The air feels breathless as her light shimmers and spreads throughout the cavern. Intense shockwaves of divine femininity envelop and soon overwhelm us.

* * *

We wake up two days later. Something is different. The Tantra Stone is whole and is spreading its energy across the planet. There is the sense of change in the air. Feelings of relief and elation flood my being. A tantric shift is long overdue.

The monk commences his teaching duties.

If men and women do not move beyond oppression and patriarchy, if they cannot ascend anger and feminism, they will never move into a new world. The Tantra Stone has sent out its call: An invitation to manifest the Divine Masculine – beyond aggression and spineless apologetic behaviour – offering presence, dignity, direction and power-in-service. And an invitation to manifest the Divine Feminine – beyond submission and fury – offering heart, intuition, connectedness and compassion.

These qualities reside within each one of us. They need to be united to create a new form of romantic partnership and a new form of leadership for our families, communities, societies and countries. It is time for change on this earth!

I have this urge to stand and applaud.

Śakra glances at me and smiles. He is acting all mysterious, like he knows something but will not share.

Chief Elder, would you like to teach us about Dreamtime?

The old man arises from his perch and moves to centre-stage. Sitting on the rock bench near the crystal pool, he strokes his beard a few times then heaves a big sigh. His eyes look weary and I imagine he has seen a lot of change in his lifetime.

"The Dreaming ... a concept often misunderstood. The word has drifted through much of Aboriginal culture and has been used to explain many things. However, its true meaning is metaphysical. One on level it refers to the creation of this world by the ancestral creation spirits. And this is true of course. But it goes much deeper than that. The Dreaming belongs to Shakti."

"Shakti?" I blurt out.

He gazes at me, his brow intensely furrowed. "Adam, the mysterious one, the one who nobody knows. What are you doing here? Why have you invaded our inner sanctum?"

Caught off guard, I stammer. "Uh ... I am part of a mission."

"What mission?"

"Um ... to help collect sacred stones ... holy objects ..."

"For what purpose? Why are you here?"

I feel trapped. No idea what to say. I am just trying to survive this adventure.

"I see you are not a dreamer."

"A dreamer?" There's that student echo again.

"What's the point of living if you have no vision? You think life is about hiding behind prayer and meditation? You think it's all about your spiritual development? What's your destination? What are you bringing to the planet? Where's your destiny?"

Ouch. Direct and confrontational. Everyone is staring at me, waiting for my response.

"I believe my old life is over. These lessons happened for a reason. It is time for me to find my path."

The chief elder looks at Śakra. "How many months until the end of the cycle?"

About five.

"I suggest you stay here during this time. You can conduct your seminars and Adam can learn to dream. These caves are an ideal way to stay off the energy grid."

Agreed.

It appears I don't have a say in the matter. I have this uncomfortable feeling ... like I need to grow up ... I wonder if this is an initiation.

Mandu takes me to one side. "Everything will be alright. All life is a progression, like the bush that grows and matures and blooms."

I nod. "Yeah, but the bush dies in the end."

"Everything dies. That is inevitable and irrelevant. It is not about your eventual death ... it's about how you are choosing to live right here, right now. Your job is to bloom – for yourself and for the world."

I shake his arm away and walk into an adjoining cavern. Need to be alone. Tired of all this compromise ... following other people's directions ... changing countries and cultures ... the push and pull of constant teaching ... jumping and adapting ... no control over my life ... no feeling of me and mine.

I sit on the dusty floor. Tears prickle my eyes then flow down my cheeks. I seldom cry ... such fatigue ... the unceasing struggle ... the loneliness ... why I am feeling this? ... there is a bigger picture ... there are planetary issues ... it is not all about me.

Perhaps I am supposed to be alone to figure this out ... Are they right? ... Do I lack vision? ... Where's my sense of personal mission? ... Where am I going? ... Am I living selfishly? ... Is it wrong to have my own desires, wants and wishes?

Śakra's words come flooding back: *Love is made of real people in real relationships that understand the necessity of compromise and sacrifice. People who know how to communicate their needs but also know how to balance the various needs in a relationship.*

It's this thing about needs, isn't it? Dreaming and introspection to bring my needs to the surface ... learning to clearly express those needs to other people ... listening to others to ascertain their needs ... discussing mutually beneficial ways to meet all our needs ... and accepting that sometimes certain needs simply cannot be met ... oh ... now I understand the context of 'compromise and sacrifice'.

What else did he say? *This life is an Adventure of the Heart. It is not about power and greed and self-serving interests. It is about entanglement in reality – real people, unguarded hearts, deep connections.*

The monk sticks his head around the corner. *It's about sharing and visioning and holding hands.*

"You finishing my thoughts now?"

He smiles. *We are walking this road together.*

"Thank you. Can you organise some clean clothes?"

I pull an apple from my bag and munch it thoughtfully. This strange place will be my home for the next few months. Better get used to it. Time to get down to some digging and self-exploration.

Laying my head on the ground, I stare into the redness. It looks like a giant cat has clawed the entire cavern ceiling. I close my eyes and let sleep wrestle with me. The last thing I remember is Śakra's ebullient expression as he voiced *The journey of Tantra is the wildest exposure of one's own heart and the most loving acceptance of another's heart.*

* * *

In the morning I awaken to find fresh clothes, a facecloth and soap placed neatly beside me. A running stream provides the opportunity for a good wash and I soon feel invigorated. Suitably attired, I make my way to the main cavern. Newcomers have been asked to bring plenty of food so breakfast has a rather cheerful atmosphere. After some time it quietens.

Śakra walks slowly into the muted light. His gaze sweeps across the audience, stopping to fix an enigmatic stare here and there. Ripping the Tantra Stone from his necklace, he holds it up for all to see. As soon as it reverts to natural size he extracts it from the silver sheath. The yantra glows brightly against the blackness of the obsidian glass.

Now that this Stone is whole, the yantra will shine forever. For those of you who arrived late: This mystical diagram holds the essence of Divine Tantra, the merging of Shiva and Shakti. The long vertical line refers to the deeper esoteric elements of Tantra while the shorter horizontal line alludes to the earthly aspects.

"I think it's time to talk about the vertical line," a voice chirps in the background.

First tell me your understanding of the horizontal line.

No one gets away lightly in the cavern. "Um, uh … our planet has a history of misaligned and disparate relationships … inequitable distribution of power … oppression, domination, subjugation … pollution and ecological damage … rape, genocide, violence and war. This has resulted from the immature masculine and the immature feminine. Thankfully there have been dramatic and notable exceptions who have brought change to our world, often at considerable cost to themselves. Now we are welcoming the

Divine Masculine and Divine Feminine and absorbing the deep beauty of these energies. This means living in a new truth, and respecting and appreciating the planet and all its beings."

He coughs, a little embarrassed. After a moment cheerful clapping fills the air.

Never forget that 'living in a new truth' requires action. It is not some theory that you merely espouse. Others change when you change. You will convert entire communities and societies when you behave in a tantric way. Words are empty. Actions count.

"And what if they hurt or reject you?"

It is only fear and pain that keep people in darkness. Shine your light and trust that it will bring transformation. What three words do you want to hold in your mind at all times?

I call out: "Courage. Forgiveness. Vulnerability."

Indeed.

Then I can't resist adding: "It's the mantra of Tantra."

Laughter peals through the cavern.

I think you are ready for the vertical elements of Tantra. This part gets a little tricky so you need to pay close attention.

There are two aspects to Life. The one is the underlying Source, the almost ubiquitous unmanifested Field of Dreams. This is represented by the god Shiva, the harbinger of death. The other is the infinite realities, the manifested dreams. This is represented by the goddess Shakti, who is both the creative force and the creation.

The Source by its very nature is invisible and impossible to encounter without experiencing your own death. Everything that is created will eventually dissolve into the Source. This is the inevitable role of Shiva.

Shakti is the one who weaves the magic cloth, who spins the universal web, who brings the dreams to life. She is the manifestation of the Source, effectively rendering the Source visible to itself.

Shiva and Shakti are the greatest Lovers. Love is when Life meets itself through creation. Love is when Life returns home to the Source. Life is breathing this Love in the eternal Now. Life is essentially one big orgasm of the Heart.

Wow, my mind is tripping.

Each one of you yearns to remember your true nature and rediscover the bliss and serenity of this Love. However, the journey is completely within your control. Every choice you make and every action you take will move you closer to or further from the Source. It's all totally up to you. No one can save you or do the work for you. You are responsible for your own journey.

"If there's an eternal Now, is there not an eternal Being?" It's Mandu, looking very serious.

Śakra smiles. *Are you sure you can handle the answer?*

"Go on ..."

There is only One Consciousness and everything is a manifestation of that Consciousness. Everything that is manifested is still the One Consciousness. Everything that exists is a Thought of God but the Thoughts also are God. Everything is One. One Being, One Moment, One Breath.

"So Shiva and Shakti are one."

Shiva and Shakti are themselves merely Thoughts of God. There is only One Consciousness. The Source is faintly understood through its symbols and manifestations. To truly know the Source, you need to die to self and swim in the One Consciousness. This is called awakening or enlightenment.

He places his hand on Mandu's shoulder. *You, my friend, are both the dream and the Dreamer.*

I glance around the room. A melange of sage nods, mumbling and mild confusion. Śakra notices it too. He twirls his hand and gives a deep bow.

Today we scratch the surface of the Mystery. Tomorrow we become immersed in it!

As he exits the cavern I burst into smile. Centuries of experience have given the monk a flair for the dramatic. Or maybe he is just a darn good story-teller. Either way, it's more than enough to contemplate. I wander into a nearby cave, find a soft place and settle into deep meditation.

* * *

The next few weeks are interesting. As usual, I adapt to the people and the new location. There is plenty of time to absorb the mystical teachings of the monk and ponder my personal vision. I am now calling this place the Labyrinth of Mystery, an epithet that the Anangu particularly enjoy. Śakra is in good form, delivering his lectures to a select group of Aboriginal people who pledge to spread the wisdom across Australia.

I can't help but wonder what is happening on the outside. What is Apophis up to? Just how popular and powerful has he become? We have remained safe and secure within the heart of Uluru but at some point we will have to emerge and face the dark ones. The thought of this inevitable encounter fills me with trepidation.

I am starting to sense a mantle of leadership falling onto my shoulders. The lessons, the mentoring, the spiritual adventure – these have been no coincidence. There is a sense of being prepared for something. Either I continue to be dragged along reluctantly like a petulant child or I surrender into the flow of events. It has nothing to do with ego and self-interest and everything to do with self-realisation and heeding the call of my destiny.

Those are lavish and grandiose thoughts.

"I know. It feels arrogant and ridiculous."

Perhaps you should start believing them. You have to learn to trust your intuition. When you meet someone for the first time, you immediately encounter their energy field. Everything you need to know about that person is written in their energy. Your misinterpretations are usually the result of the mind's interference – assumptions and projections. You often get hurt when you ignore the intuitive voice – the voice of your soul. Equally, you are living and breathing in a Field of Energy which contains plenty of helpful information, including the whispers from the multi-dimensions. Learn to tap and absorb these messages.

"How do I do this?"

Keep meditating as it naturally cultivates your sensitivity. Commit to living with impeccability. Align yourself with the beings of light that exist everywhere and everywhen. Great power results from initiating such an allegiance.

"Tell me more."

First we have to meet the shamans. The next part of our journey is about to commence.

A knot immediately forms in my stomach. "Are we leaving?"

Have you seen the date? It's January 2027 – the next cycle has begun.

Why am I filled with such dread?

Śakra looks kindly at me. *We'll make it through this together.*

A modicum of relief. "Where are we going?"

South Africa. We leave in the morning.

* * *

I didn't know South Africa had shamans.

We have arrived in a beautiful country on the southern tip of Africa, embraced by the cool Atlantic Ocean on the west and the warm Indian Ocean on the east. The monk has landed us on the beach and it is tempting to run into the waves and disappear for an hour.

To my surprise, however, Ra and Baset are waiting for us. I swallow hard. This must mean trouble. It's been over three years since I have seen the sun-god. I barely know him. Does he shake hands?

He bows cordially. *Adam, good to see you. Has the monk taught you well?*

I can't resist. "Indeed."

A faint flicker of a smile. I am sure he knows anyway.

We jump into the waiting 4x4. Nominated as driver, I get down to planning the route. We are situated in the iSimangaliso Wetland Park at St Lucia, an exquisite subtropical paradise hugging the east coast. Ra has circled the destination on a map: Ulundi, in the province of KwaZulu-Natal. It is four hours inland in a south-westerly direction.

Śakra is sitting next to me. "What's in Ulundi?"

The shaman.

He says nothing more. In fact, he has been remarkably quiet since we greeted the sun-god. Is he respectfully deferring to the authority of Ra? Or is something on his mind? We drive in silence. Apart from the engine the only other noise is the loud purring of Baset on the back seat.

After a couple of hours I've had enough. "Will someone please tell me where we are going?"

Ra stirs. *eMakhosini, meaning Place of the Kings, near Ulundi. It is the heart of the Zulu nation and contains many sacred sites in its hills and valleys.*

It goes quiet again. I sigh. "Who are the Zulu?"

The Zulu are the largest South African ethnic group, living mainly in the province of KwaZulu-Natal. The word Zulu means 'heaven' or 'sky' and they are often referred to as the sky people.

It's going to be a long day. I wipe my brow. The warm, very humid weather is making me pour with sweat. My shirt is sticking to my back.

Expansive green grasslands come into view. We pass a few dome-shaped huts. A low-hanging fluffy white cloud has draped itself mysteriously over the area. Ra points out a hill in the distance. *That's where we are going.*

A Zulu male in traditional dress is standing by the side of the road. He raises his spear indicating that we should halt. Not a word is exchanged but it is clear that we must follow him. Soon we encounter a large thatched hut residing in the shade of a huge Amarula tree. A stream trickles nearby.

The atmosphere feels spooky and the hairs on my arms are raised. Suddenly a piercing scream fills the air. Moments later a woman emerges, staggering and smiling.

Śakra leans toward me. *The sangoma has just extracted dark energy from her. Part of the healing process.*

"Sangoma?"

South African shamans are called sangomas. They work with the ancestral spirits to gain information, do healings and counteract dark energy. They are very powerful.

Half an hour goes by. A sunbird slowly preens in the shade of the Amarula. I stoop to run my fingers through the cool stream. Nature provides a welcome distraction from my apprehension.

Finally the door of the hut flings open to reveal the sangoma. She is wearing an ornate beaded headdress and strips of animal skin crisscross her chest. Her necklace contains a cluster of small containers filled with various herbs. She is shaking a cow-tail whisk in her right hand. It's all rather intimidating until a broad smile creases her face.

"Śakra!" The slight monk is quickly engulfed in a stocky affectionate hug.

She looks over at Ra. "Ah, the sun-god. What took you so long? We could have used your presence years ago."

Ra shifts uncomfortably. The energy field becomes thick with tension. It feels … angry … wait, ignore my mind … a member of the Council of Light … she knows the monk well … comforted him when he was grieving … a lost love … the gods were called upon and failed to show.

A burst of sadness flows through my heart and is quickly followed by a flame of fury. Where are these feelings coming from? Are they mine?

I look at Śakra. "Were you in love with the Guardian of the Earth?" My words cut through the strained ambience.

The finger slowly raises to point at Ra as the blood rushes to his face. The moment lasts forever. Then he turns away and walks off into the bush.

The sangoma's countenance is stern and kind. "Did you ever apologise to that boy?"

The sun-god shrugs his shoulders. He looks like a parent who has made a monumental mistake with his child and has no idea how to sort the matter. Even the gods are fallible.

Beckoning to Ra, she says "Come, we need to talk."

"Um, I'm Adam."

"Yes, Adam, I know who you are. We'll see you later."

That leaves me and the mute Zulu warrior. I make myself comfortable under the tree and watch the butterflies flitting overhead. It's a good thing I like solitude.

* * *

"Iboga."

I open my eyes. "Huh?"

"My name is Iboga. I am a visionary shaman, trained to get to the root of spiritual matters."

"Pleased to meet you."

"What's so special about you?"

"What do you mean?"

She transfixes me with her penetrating stare. "Why are you here? What do you want?"

I feel like I am back in the Labyrinth of Mystery.

"I am a leader ... um, a leader-in-training ..."

She bursts out laughing then raises one eyebrow. "Oh really?"

I swallow. This woman is actually quite scary.

"Fear will not serve you, Adam Kadmon. Now tell me, what do you know of the multi-dimensions?"

"Um ... nothing ..."

"Then how will you lead anyone? There are many who are erudite, many who are eloquent, many who are persuasive, but few have travelled the multi-dimensions."

She shouts toward the hut. "Ra, you need to leave this one with me."

I quiver slightly. My mind races for an excuse. "What about Apophis?"

"That dark lizard! He is too busy plotting the overthrow of governments and the destruction of the Light to worry about you."

"No, I mean shouldn't we be chasing him?"

"Wait until your enemy comes to you. Let's see his hand first."

What was the lesson from Tantra? Courage and vulnerability. "I am ready to learn from you. Please take good care of me." I look at the ground for a moment. It turns out that it's really not that difficult to express my needs.

"Of course."

She is standing with her hands on her hips, gazing at me. "I don't think we are going to see Śakra for a while. He loved the Guardian for more than a thousand years. That's some grief. Let's have dinner and you can go relax. You will be staying in the village across the way."

Ra is pretty subdued even with Baset purring around his feet. I guess we are all on a journey and we are all learning. Iboga is a gracious host full of interesting conversation. With the onset of dusk we stroll over to the village and settle in our new homes. As I lay my head on the pillow, an image of the heartbroken monk flashes in my mind. A millennium – that's a whole lot of love.

* * *

Over the next few months Iboga takes me on repeated and intense inner journeys. This is not as simple as meditation, rather it involves a confrontation and appreciation of the various aspects of my soul. Unfortunately it also brings me close to my deepest fears and anxieties. No matter how much bravado I carry and no matter how I try to philosophise, it becomes obvious that I fear my own death. Perhaps we all do.

The sangoma is holding my hand. "It is not the loss of your physical body that concerns you but the loss of your self, your identity, your you-ness."

Every now and then I encounter a brightly coloured swirling tunnel. For some reason this scares me and I refuse to enter it. There are countless doors peppering the walls of the tunnel. I surmise these are access points to the multi-dimensions.

She consoles me. "You will go when you are ready. Each person moves in their own time."

I glance at the small bush with its pink and white flowers and elongated orange fruit. Śakra's recent words filter into my consciousness: *Every choice you make and every action you take will move you closer to or further from the Source. It's all totally up to you. No one can save you or do the work for you. You are responsible for your own journey.*

Each time I return to earthly reality I have great difficulty explaining my experiences. This despairing and joyful exploration into the layers of my being. This uncovering and unveiling of my innermost essence. How can anyone truly understand the curvatures of another's soul?

It makes me think about the inevitable loneliness of life. We were all born and we are all going to die. We cannot explain how we came to exist. Nor can we be certain about the realms beyond physical death. All we know is that we have choices in this life. And that each person's journey is their own.

Individual spirits are surfing solitary threads of light on their way back to the Source. However, we can reach out to each other and hold hands. It may be impossible to fully experience another's life but we can connect through warm conversations, gentle touches, soft words, kind smiles and the flicker of love that dances in our eyes.

My life becomes a melange of stumbling into the hut at night or just sleeping in the bush, sometimes I awaken in the cradle of a beautiful tree, the spectres of my soul haunting me, my own darkness drifting past, the fierce grip of insight shaking me to my roots, the purge of beliefs that no longer serve me, the agonising sweat of personal history, the reminders of could-have should-have if-only, and the long slow awakening to possibilities, to ideas, to responsibility, the shift toward a different way of being.

One fine day Śakra appears and joins me on a journey. The cracked barren landscape rushes up to meet us ... sun beating down ... hot ... thirsty ... struggling ... tears spatter the ground and a tiny sapling spirals into view ... rippling grey light ... the rage of thunder and menacing clouds ... overnight the long grass grows ... an enormous tree covers us with custodial boughs ... enough ... something greater than both of us ... surrender brings serenity ... brilliant rays peeping over the horizon ... acceptance of the past ... forgiveness ... letting go ... moving forward ...

Courage. Forgiveness. Vulnerability.

"What?" I stir in the bushes and glance over at the monk.

It's all Tantra, isn't it? The Way of the Heart.

"Are you back?"

He smiles. *Yep.*

"I'm hungry."

Me too.

We trundle over to the sangoma's hut and knock on the door. She emerges, then slowly walks around us with an appraising eye. "Yes ... much better ... we may yet be able to make something of you." I am not sure who she is talking about. She shoos us away. "Come back for breakfast in an hour. And go have a wash!"

* * *

The day is warm and sunny. Thankfully the humidity has dropped. I feel completely renewed and peaceful. Ra and Śakra are talking quietly in the corner. That's a good sign.

Iboga calls us to the table. "After breakfast you should check the newsfeed. You are going to want to see what's happened." We eat hurriedly, clean the dishes and switch on the sangoma's lume.

'July 2027. A devastating earthquake has wrenched the Temple Mount in Jerusalem, completely demolishing both the al-Aqsa Mosque and the Dome of the Rock and levelling much of the city. People around the world are grieving. One of the biggest shocks has come from the leader of the World Peace Organisation, Apophis. He is calling it an omen – a message that we need to turn away from antiquated religious practices and put our faith in the political leaders of this world.'

"Wow. Did Apophis make that happen?"

Ra looks up. *Absolutely.*

"Are we going to do something?"

We cannot act until he shows the world his true colours.

"This is just the beginning, isn't it?"

A horrible feeling grips my stomach. I read the energy field. "There's a dark one nearby."

Ra nods and places a finger over his lips. We slip out of the hut and hide in the bushes. There are two of them – one thirty metres away, the other concealing itself against a distant rock. Baset disappears to cover the flank.

There is no visible airship. They must be on reconnaissance. Apophis has probably despatched teams of scouts across the planet. We need to eliminate them quietly.

The pine cone on the Staff of Light is glowing softly. We wait for the optimal position. Ra takes aim and the cone erupts into fiery fragments, then reforms and cools. The dark one didn't stand a chance. In the background a familiar ferocious whirl as Baset attacks the second scout. Her fangs and claws glimmer against the dark adversary. I shiver in admiration. That cat can move!

Ra walks into the open. *It's all good. They had no time to contact anyone. We are safe for now.*

"What's the agenda of the Dark Lizard?"

Take over the world. Subjugate free will. Destroy the Light.

"Increase the power of the dark lattice."

Precisely.

"Do you mind if I take the rest of the day –"

Whatever you need.

I excuse myself and return to the village. A bit of everyday distraction and interaction with ordinary people will do me some good. It's been a busy few months and I need to escape for a while.

* * *

"All this sitting around is driving me crazy. How can we just wait for Apophis to make the first move? Suppose he sends more scouts … or hunters."

Śakra leans over. *Chill out, dude. Baset can see in the multidimensions. She is monitoring the situation.*

"You're a surfer now?"

I've lived in a few places. Carved a few waves.

"Yeah, you've been around a long time."

I want to ask him about the Guardian of the Earth. What did she look like? When did he fall in love with her? I wonder if it's a sensitive topic.

The monk appears lost in thought. He gets up and picks a wild flower. *Love was inevitable. Two similar beings on a long-term mission. Engaged in secret work. A gradual evolution of our knowledge and wisdom. She became more beautiful with each passing decade.* He smiles. *We argued so much in the beginning. She was stubborn and quick-tempered and fiercely independent; later I discovered this was simply an aspect of her great passion.*

"I guess you can fall in love for many reasons."

Love is a two-edged sword that requires courage and vulnerability. The longer and deeper you love and the more you surrender into it, the greater your immersion into deep happiness and joy and the greater the potential for pain through loss. Her death cut me to the core.

"I'm sorry. Where is she now?"

In another dimension. We see each other sometimes but it's not the same. It's like loving someone who lives in another country.

"Was it worth it?"

You know the answer to that one. Love is always worth it.

My heart feels all warm. The sun breaks through the clouds, creating a fan of soft beams. An expansive flock of chirping birds swoops overhead. I gaze in awe as the choreographed troupe dances cheerfully across the sky.

"Hang on … how do you see each other?"

The answer lies in the multi-dimensions.

"Oh yeah. I haven't quite got there yet."

You will. When you stop being such a scaredy-cat.

A strong hiss emanates from the bushes.

Oh, sorry … when you stop being such a chicken.

He tucks his hands into his armpits and raises his elbows. He walks around flapping his arms and bobbing his head. *Puck, puck, pu-uck, pu-uck!*

"Iboga! We need you over here. Śakra is having a fit!"

The sangoma comes running over, takes one look at the monk and slaps me on the arm with the cow-tail whisk. Ouch!

"Don't you boys have anything better to do?"

Puck, pu –

"Śakra!"

We fall into laughter then take flight across the grassland. As we follow the path back to the village I have this sudden realisation: We are becoming good friends. A smile lights up my face. Now I just need to master the multi-dimensions.

* * *

The sun is bright in the sky. All around me I hear the sounds of nature waking up. A soft breeze caresses my shoulders. It's going to be another magnificent day.

Iboga has clients all morning so we keep ourselves busy and stay out of her way. After lunch we sit down together in the shade of the Amarula.

"Do you understand what sangomas do?"

"Yep. You work with the ancestral spirits to gain information, do healings and counteract dark energy."

"The Zulu term Nkunku lu means First to Emerge and refers to God as creator and sustainer of the universe. Many call this the Source or the Fountain of Life. We cannot communicate directly with the Source but with enough training we can connect to the ancestors. The ancestors are beings who have walked this earth but now reside in another dimension. They are always willing to assist the earthly realm."

"That makes sense. All this talk of God and gods and ancestors confuses me."

"God is the Source, the underlying Is-ness, the Creator of everything. A deep ocean that gives rise to infinite waves. Your reality is merely one of these waves."

"There is nothing but the Source and the multi-dimensions?"

"At this level of understanding – yes."

Śakra smiles. *You need to remember that these dimensions are not layers but expressions of Life. Hence they manifest in countless ways. Your perception limits you to the terms 'physical' and 'spiritual'. Life, however, expresses itself in unlimited configurations and forms.*

"Does that make surfing the multi-dimensions rather challenging? Is that why the Aborigines and sangomas work mostly with the ancestors?"

Yes. The ancestors are beings who have a connection and commitment to earth. They are the ideal ones to ask for help. Occasionally a few of the ancestors move on to other dimensions and new ones take their place. All life is a journey, a progression and a gradual return to the Source.

Wow. These are such fundamental teachings. "Why should I learn to surf the multi-dimensions?"

You can do whatever you choose. Stay in this reality. Enjoy life, find love, live your dreams. Or you can explore the countless other realities. There are so many opportunities. It is completely up to you.

The sangoma steps in. "For too long this world has divorced consciousness from science, democracy from politics, compassion from economic policy, and the multi-dimensions from religion. The more you understand your own nature and your position in a boundless universe, the more you will be able to contribute to society and the world."

I lay outstretched on the grass and stare into the heavens. My life has taken so many unusual turns over the last four years. What's one more adventure?

I sigh. "When do we start?"

The only way to experience the Vortex of Life is under the guidance of an experienced spiritual teacher or shaman. You cannot do it by yourself.

Iboga gets up. "Come with me."

I stand up and sense a change in the energy field. An emanation from the sangoma's hut. It's the Staff of Light. The pine cone is glowing again. I cast my mind back to when I first met Ra and we discussed the staff. He explained: *It focuses the light. Light can be used as a weapon; it can be used to communicate with other realms; and it can open the consciousness to the multi-dimensions.*

"Wait. We need the Staff of Light. It's a shortcut to the vortex."

Iboga looks at me. "So now you want to go in the deep end. I thought you were scared."

"I am. But I need to be pushed over the edge. Besides, I know you will look after me."

She walks into the hut and has a word with Ra. A few minutes later she has the staff in her hand. Impressive. Who else could convince the sun-god to give up his weapon?

"Sit against the tree and close your eyes. Both Śakra and I will be with you, though you may not immediately be aware of us."

I sense the warmth of the pine cone as it touches my forehead. Instantaneously a shining door appears in front of me. This is no hallucination. I look around. There is nothing but dark blue shimmering energy and this portal before me. I have been transported to another world.

With some trepidation I pull the door open. And there it is. The huge pulsating vortex with spiralling bright colours and millions of exits. Taking a deep breath, I leap inside.

The noise is intense. All I can hear is an extremely loud scchhh! as if enormous electrical wires are crossing. It is completely disorienting. I feel overwhelmed and sick. Śakra grabs my arm. *Focus. This is nothing but the mind's reaction. Feel the energy.*

I grasp the nearest door and hurtle into a purple dusk. There are tents everywhere. I stumble to the campfire and sit down. "It looks like we have a visitor." I try hard to focus. Long black hair with a silver streak down the side. Native American? "You're early – we're due to meet in 2028." He laughs. "Glad to see you are practising." Horses are neighing. Water cascades nearby.

It's getting blurry. Can't hold on. "Leaving so soon?" He looks past my shoulder. I turn around. There's the exit. I jump through and tumble into the bright colours.

It seems a bit calmer. Am I adjusting to the noise? I stand up and run over the crisscrossing lines. Here's a door covered in pink hearts. Why not? Falling into a huge feather bed … white pillows … antique furniture … brushing her long auburn hair in front of the mirror … she turns … "Hey, sleepy head!" … bounds onto the bed and scatters kisses all over my face … her blue eyes luminous in the soft light. I am home. Where I belong. Tears streak down my cheeks. There's a framed photo on the bedside table. I feel so loved.

I bounce upward through the ceiling and return to the vortex. How do I control this? I recall the Sikh and the gushing river where I used to meditate. Ah, the calm still centre. I settle my energy and find the detached observer. Is this vortex me? Are we connected in some way? The doors are slowing ... or am I slowing?

A dark portal presents itself. I hear the monk's voice. *You are not ready to go in there.* I push the door. It is clammy and oppressive, feels hard to breathe, great sadness and rage, blindness, agony seeping from the walls, terrible fear and pain. I slump to the ground. A dark being rubs its slithery fingers over my forehead. I scream ... powerless ... hopeless ... no point being alive ... nothing matters ... disappearing in the isolation ... the emptiness ... a glowing flicker ... the monk in my periphery ... needle of light flying through the dark ... another scream ... dazzling plumes ... the door ... escape ...

I pause inside the pulsating vortex. How do I get home? Focus ... think of my reality ... beautiful green and blue door ... jump through. Open my eyes. My body spasms violently. Steady myself against the tree. Unable to speak, then "Is this my world?"

Śakra and Iboga are seated next to me. I am safe. I am home.

* * *

You weren't kidding about the deep end!

"Is there another way?"

You usually warm up with a few innocuous realities then graduate to the more serious stuff.

"You didn't mention that."

Am I in control of your journey now?

"Where was I anyway?"

From your perspective, you visited the future.

"Were those actual realities?"

You want the entire lecture again?

I feel disturbed. "Why was the darkness in the Vortex of Life?"

Śakra rolls his eyes. *This is why you need a guide in the beginning. Connecting to the ancestors is relatively safe and easy. If you want to explore other dimensions, anything can happen. Hence the term 'mastering the multi-dimensions'.*

"How was the dark one defeated?"

First of all, through alignment with the beings of light that exist everywhere and everywhen. Remember we spoke about this? Great power results from such an allegiance. Secondly, through knowing one's own true nature. Thirdly, because of impeccable living. Also, I have the Dart of Light.

"That flying needle?"

He pulls it from his necklace. Five centimetres, wafer-thin, glistening like diamond.

You need to use it strategically as it strikes only one target at a time. It is very powerful. Read its energy.

"Its energy?"

Come on. You can do this.

"Yes, with living beings ..."

Everything is energy. Everything is consciousness.

"Have you taught me that before?"

I hope so.

"Ok ... sense the energy ... ah ... 'resistance is futile' ..."

That was easy. Why the big fuss?

I shrug. "Can I read anything?"

Of course. Do you understand the dart's power now?

"Tiny but irresistible?"

Exactly.

"How many sacred objects were left on the earth?"

Twelve.

I feel my necklace. I am carrying the Adi Shakti, the Vajra, the Bell and the Koan. The monk has the Tantra Stone, the Phoenix, the Loophole and the Dart. The sun-god has the Staff of Light. That's nine.

"What happened to the Mezuzah?"

The water-goddess delivered it to Ra but he still doesn't know its function.

"So that's ten of the twelve objects."

Impressive counting.

"Did you follow me into all the doors?"

No. The other two had gentle energy. Why?

"No reason."

Next time try to sense the energy of the reality before you step into it.

"When is next time?"

Up to you. It's your journey.

"How about tomorrow?"

Ok. Are you finished with all the questions?

"Yep."

Let's get some dinner.

* * *

We wake up in the morning to an ash-filled sky. I walk outside. The local people are looking around in wonderment. It appears that a massive fire has raged overnight, destroying nearly everything in its path; however, the village is completely untouched.

I run to the sangoma's hut. All the plant life in a hundred-metre radius is pristine. Iboga is sitting on a bench, threading beads onto her headdress. I ask if she is alright. A deep furrow knits her brow. "That crafty old lizard cannot destroy my village." Unbelievable. No wonder sangomas have such a formidable reputation.

We share breakfast then check the newsfeed. Devastating fires are blazing around the globe. Hard for governments to explain under 'natural causes'. Australia is battling infernos across its states and territories. Numerous temples and shrines in Japan have been razed. China is struggling to save sacred Confucian and Buddhist sites. Remarkably, nothing is happening in the Middle East and Europe. Apophis is quiet too. He undoubtedly has a long-term strategy.

Over the next few weeks Ra spends a lot of time conferring with the Council of Light. Śakra participates in many of these discussions. I am never asked to attend, yet the cat is invited. It is quite obvious where I sit in the hierarchy.

I readily accept all opportunities to surf the multi-dimensions. There is much to explore and learn. The years of meditation practice have proven useful. It becomes clear that the key to controlling the vortex is the detached observer and the calm still centre. The second important key is the power of intention. As the monk eloquently states: *You are consciousness and your intention directs your journey.* The vortex is a curious dichotomy of my will and surrender to something far greater than me. A perfect reflection of life.

It is coming to the end of an eventful year. The sangoma is satisfied with my progress. Sitting me down under the Amarula tree one morning, she says "Let me tell you about Ubuntu."

Śakra walks by and asks to join us. I nod amiably.

"Ubuntu is a philosophy, an attitude, a way of life. Essentially it focuses on the power of relationships and allegiances. At an earthly level, this refers to keeping your connections clear of negative energy, living with forgiveness and loving-kindness, understanding that we are not alone in the Mystery, and working together for the benefit of humanity and our planet."

This is what I mean by 'living with impeccability'.

"Ah, clarity at last."

"The modern world places too much emphasis on individualism, independence and self-sufficiency. This is not the natural way to live and it results in people feeling isolated and alone. The truth is we need each other. We need each other for friendship, for romance, for effective partnerships, and to create close-knit communities and societies. Our souls are primed for connection, compassion and companionship, and we will never be truly happy unless we live with altruism."

"Altruism?"

Selfless concern for the well-being of others.

"Wow. I don't know if I am there yet."

You don't remember risking your life to save mine?

"Yes ..."

We weren't even friends back then.

I smile. "Are you saying we are friends now?"

Śakra's eyes glint in the sunlight. *Maybe.*

I slap him on the arm and laugh.

The sangoma frowns at the interruption. "As I was saying, Ubuntu focuses on relationships and allegiances. This applies to realms beyond the earth too. All sangomas make connections with the ancestors. It is our trademark. The more powerful and wise sangomas also forge alliances with the beings of light in the multi-dimensions."

I nod. "And this is why travelling those other realities is so important."

"What we are doing is nothing new. This has been done for thousands of years. Unfortunately, oppressive political and religious regimes have continually tried to wipe out these practices. And appropriate power for themselves. The dark lattice has a strong hold on this planet."

I am starting to understand the deeper nature of spirit, spirituality and religion. It's incredible how this information has been hidden from ordinary people. I have a strong sense that change is coming to our planet ... we will create a new world ... a world of love, light, freedom and spiritual power. It's going to be magnificent.

Iboga looks kindly at me. "Walk strong, Adam. These teachings will serve you well."

"That sounds suspiciously like a goodbye."

"Yes, you will be moving on soon."

"No! I don't want to lose you." My reaction completely surprises me.

"The woman waiting for you is strong-willed, courageous, vulnerable and full of love. She lives with a wide open heart accepting whatever life offers her. A wonderful partner to build a new world."

The sangoma gets to her feet. "Śakra, go fetch the sun-god."

Taking the cue, I stand as well. Suddenly I am engulfed in a massive hug. "Everything will be alright," she assures me. I whisper a thank you and sigh deeply. I am going to miss her nurturing energy.

The monk returns with Ra and Baset. *What is it, Iboga?*

She lays an animal hide on the ground and unties a large pouch. Beckoning the four of us to sit in a circle, she closes her eyes. The energy field becomes electric. "The ancestors are here. It is time to throw the bones." With a deft turn of the wrist, twenty-four bones are scattered onto the hide.

It goes quiet for a while, then "One of you will die for love. One of you will be sorely tempted. One of you will be seriously injured. Read the scripture etched onto the Mezuzah – it's your only hope of getting home."

It's a reading! A prediction of the future. Are we allowed to ask questions?

"What is the function of the Mezuzah?"

"Turn each end and count to three, and soon you'll have a master key."

Sweet. An enigmatic poem.

Ra asks the next question. *Where's the eleventh sacred object?*

"Area 51, Nevada."

That mysterious air force base in North America?

A gust of wind shrieks across the bones. There's that cold feeling again. Dark ones are approaching.

We look across the blackened fields. Three of them walking in a triangular formation. *Hunters! Adam, take the left flank. Śakra, the right. Here, use my staff. I will draw them in. Activate your weapons only after the first strike.*

Ra moves away from the hut and walks across the grassland. A warning shot is fired. He raises his hands and falls to his knees. Baset purrs sweetly as a dark one approaches. The rear guard is falling perfectly into position for a pincer movement.

The cat moves around the sun-god and everything blurs. I activate the Adi Shakti and turn the spindles of the Vajra, firing a few times. The monk despatches the searing scales of the pine cone. It is over in seconds.

We run to join Ra. *We have used too much energy. It will expose our location and endanger Iboga. Prepare to leave.*

I turn to look back at the sangoma's hut as Śakra pulls the silver circle from his necklace. A large rhinoceros with menacing horns is standing under the Amarula. I feel the blend of protective and nurturing energy. Could it be?

The Loophole opens and we all make the leap.

* * *

Like seasoned travellers we land casually and take in our surroundings. A waterfall is cascading into an exquisite turquoise pool surrounded by willows and cottonwoods and towering red sandstone cliffs. The cloudless sky is the lightest blue. "Did we just arrive in paradise?"

The monk smiles. *Havasu Falls.*

"Where exactly are we?"

Coconino County, north central Arizona, United States of America. This county contains the Grand Canyon National Park, the Havasupai Nation and parts of the Navajo Nation, Hualapai Nation and Hopi Nation.

"Native Americans?"

Yep. Havasu Canyon is a paradisiacal gorge and side branch of the Grand Canyon. The Grand Canyon itself is over 400 km long, varies between 16-29 km across and is 1.6 km deep. Awe-inspiring and impressive.

"So what are we doing here?"

This is the home of the Havasupai. Hopefully we'll meet them.

"Can you tell me more?"

Havasupai means 'people of the blue-green waters'. The Havasupai tribe is the smallest Indian Nation in America, comprising about 600 people. Historically they farmed along Havasu Creek in the summer and hunted deer, antelope and small game in the winter. They were renowned for their fine quality buck skins, powdered red ochre and beautiful basketry.

"Did anyone bring food? I'm hungry."

Dude, are you always hungry?

"Are you calling me 'dude' again?"

Why not? California is just west of here.

The monk unpacks sandwiches and water.

"Where did you get those from?"

Iboga. She has amazing precognition.

The four of us sit by the turquoise pool and enjoy a light snack. Baset scampers off into the undergrowth. I am always apprehensive when she does that; perhaps she is hunting for her own lunch. After fifteen minutes she returns, gently teasing and prodding a huge toad in our direction.

"What on earth is that?"

Ra scrutinises it. *Bufo alvarius, the Sonoran Desert Toad. Baset will not harm it. She knows it is sacred.*

"A sacred toad? Really?"

The Sonoran Desert Toad or Colorado River Toad is usually found in the lower Colorado River and the Gila River catchment areas in south-eastern California, southern Arizona, New Mexico and Mexico. It is the largest native toad in the United States and can grow up to 19 centimetres long. It is nocturnal and semi-aquatic so there is probably a family residing near this pool.

A rustle among the trees draws our attention. We have company. Śakra springs to his feet and rushes over to meet the small group. Enthusiastic greetings make it clear that these are old friends. I wonder if they are members of the Council of Light.

Adam, these four people each represent the Navajo, the Hopi, the Hualapai and the Havasupai. The fifth person is a Hopi mystic.

Nods all round. They do not seem surprised to see Ra and Baset. This meeting was probably scheduled weeks ago; there are no coincidences when you keep company with the gods.

I am not sure if I am welcome here. The monk quickly intervenes. *While these four consult with Ra, Qaletaqa will take you on a mystical journey. A journey so sacred that I may not speak of it. His name means 'guardian of the people' and he will take good care of you.*

"What are you going to do?"

It's January and it's going to get cold. I need to build a campfire for the night. Don't worry, I'll be nearby.

The Indians move off and begin unpacking the horses, pitching tents and moving various stones into a circle. Śakra is diligently collecting wood and I elect to join him. By the time the sun sets, a warm fire is crackling. I look around at the visitors relaxing in the purple dusk.

My eyes widen. Across the circle – it's me, disoriented and confused! The long black hair with a silver streak down the side belongs to the Hopi mystic! I watch myself leap through the portal. Qaletaqa turns and smiles. "I believe it is 2028 – are you ready now?" I burst out laughing. What is real? What is reality?

We fetch a few blankets then walk deep into the trees. Once we are seated, he says "Let me tell you about the Hopi. The name Hopituh Shi-nu-mu means 'the peaceful people' or 'peaceful little ones'. The Hopi strive to live in harmony with nature and all living beings, and our sacred ceremonies are conducted to benefit the entire planet."

He looks at the ground for a few moments. Is he recalling a sad memory?

"Our reservation is entirely surrounded by the extensive Navajo Reservation which stretches across north-eastern Arizona, south-eastern Utah and north-western New Mexico. Most of the 7,000 Hopi people are farmers, artists and craftsmen; we are particularly known for our fine turquoise and silver jewellery."

Loud piercing calls begin ripping through the air. "What the –"

"Sonoran Desert toads. Noisy little creatures. Are you ready to rock 'n roll?"

"Are you allowed to use phrases like that?"

"You wanted something more mystical?"

"Please."

"Ok, put your hands on your knees, palms up, thumb and forefinger touching. Keep your spine relaxed and straight. Close your eyes."

For a brief millisecond the doors of the multi-coloured vortex flash through my consciousness. Then with no advance warning I am catapulted straight into the Light. Quite simply, I cease to exist.

After twenty minutes I return to earth and discover that I am splayed out on the ground like a dishevelled rag doll.

We take a short break to discuss the experience. I adopt the posture and try again. This time I am rocketed past ethereal veils, directly into twinkling stars scattered across the dark cosmos. Soon a glorious pulsating sun swallows me. My memories disappear and mad laughter peals through the universe.

When I come to, I am flat on my back with the blanket thrown to one side.

I look at the Hopi mystic. "What's the point of starting these journeys with a special posture?"

Qaletaqa gazes at me. "Do you need rituals, mantras and poses to experience the Truth?"

"Obviously not."

"Actually it depends. Some people prefer the slow circuitous route. Not everyone is ready to directly access the Light."

The night is getting cold so we amble back to the campfire and join the light-hearted discussion. I am completely bereft of words. My mind is still floating in the heavens. It is not long before we are safely ensconced in our warm tents. Sleep envelops me quickly.

A month of powerful journeys, secret teachings and campfire conversations passes quickly. In February the Indians depart. I give my heartfelt thanks to the Hopi mystic. He smiles enigmatically. "This is neither our first nor our last meeting."

The four of us huddle around a blazing fire. I suggest a location near Area 51. After some discussion the monk hands me the silver circle. We jump tomorrow. Bright lights, tall buildings and abundant neon signs. Las Vegas, here we come!

* * *

It's a good decision. The buzzing Vegas energy grid renders us practically invisible to the dark ones. Trading a couple of rough diamonds allows us to rent a small house on the outskirts of the city for three months. We negotiate the chores. I don't mind running the washing machine or driving the 4x4 but cooking is definitely not my forte.

Turns out that Śakra is a brilliant chef. I guess you learn a few things when you've been alive that long. I volunteer to do the food shopping and we quickly relax into a routine.

The newsfeed continues to surprise us. Apophis is remarkably quiet which makes it all the more ominous. What is he planning? His popularity and power continue to grow, particularly within countries covered by the World Peace Organisation.

Over breakfast one morning I ask Ra "What are we waiting for? How long are we staying in Vegas?"

Our time in Havasu Falls was well spent. I was thoroughly briefed about Area 51 but I am still waiting for a vital piece of information. It is probably time for you to catch up.

"I am listening."

Area 51 is a top secret military base located in southern Nevada, about 230 kilometres north of our current location. The base lies within the United States Air Force's vast Nevada Test and Training Range (NTTR), formerly called the Nellis Air Force Range (NAFR). Its purpose is to develop and test experimental aircraft and weapon systems.

"I am sure there are operations like that all over the world."

A large military airfield with runways is positioned on the southern shore of Groom Lake. However, most of the action takes place underground inside the Papoose Mountain Range near Papoose Lake.

"What action?"

The storage and analysis of alien artefacts and spacecraft.

"You mean like Apophis' airships?"

Yes. Project Dreamland is a joint venture involving many countries. It was initiated to defend your planet against malign alien forces. Scientists desperately attempt to reverse-engineer various off-world objects in order to assimilate knowledge and create advanced defensive technology. Information is highly classified and the base is heavily protected.

"Eminently sensible."

There are two issues. Firstly, many people on earth are frustrated by the secretive nature of Project Dreamland and want the truth about alien spacecraft shared openly. Secondly, the dark masters who control worldwide political, economic, religious and media power want this information suppressed. If people discover the truth it will seriously undermine the dark lattice.

"The truth will out."

Shakespeare?

I nod. "Project Dreamland sounds interesting."

It also incorporates the study of recovered bodies from alien crash sites; hybridisation experiments; meetings with beings from other dimensions or 'extraterrestrials'; and the development of weather control, energy weapons and exotic propulsion systems.

"How do they keep it so secret?"

Through state-of-the-art surveillance technology, shadowy military control and superb camouflage. The airspace around Groom Lake is severely restricted. Radar stations protect the skies; cameras and buried motion sensors monitor the land. Private armed security guards in Humvees and SUVs patrol the perimeter. Deadly force is authorised if trespassers attempt to breach the secured area.

"And you want us to break into this base?"

Not yet. I still don't know what we are looking for.

"Have you scanned the energy grid over Area 51?"

Baset is doing this right now. Nothing is showing.

"When Śakra and I found the Mezuzah, we could get no signal either. It was hidden beneath the ground. Probably like the eleventh sacred object. We just took a chance and jumped through the Loophole."

Ra looks thoughtful. *This facility is protected by sophisticated detection and defence systems. Also, not one of us have been there before.*

I tuck my hands into my armpits and raise my elbows. "Puck, puck, pu-uck, pu-uck!"

A cushion flies across the room toward me. I rapidly exit the kitchen and go outside for some fresh air. Why am I helping him anyway? Breaking into Area 51 will make Mecca seem like a walk in the park. Do we really need to disturb another hornets' nest?

* * *

"I am tired of sitting around!"

Ra looks at me over the unfolded map.

"Śakra once said *There is a time for stillness, a time for strategizing and a time for action. Wisdom is knowing when each of these should be applied.* Stillness is not going to bring us any more information. It's time for action."

He nods. *What do you propose?*

"It's already late May. The lease is about to expire. Let's get up to Area 51 and scout around."

Ok, perhaps we will learn something. Baset already has the layout of Papoose Mountain.

"When do we leave?"

How fast can you make sandwiches?

I rush through the kitchen and pack the car, ensuring that we have plenty of water. By eleven we are moving north on Route 93. As usual the monk is in front with me. Baset is leaning over the side of the vehicle, catching the wind and creating peculiar faces. I don't know if she is trying to be funny but soon we are in stitches.

Śakra leans toward me. *Where are we headed?*

I have been planning this for weeks. "To a small town called Rachel, the closest habitation to Area 51. Here's the best part: I have booked us rooms at the Little A'Le'Inn motel for the entire month of June. It has an alien-themed restaurant and bar and sells extraterrestrial souvenirs."

The monk raises an eyebrow. *Seriously?*

"We may as well enjoy ourselves."

It takes about ninety minutes to drive Route 93, then we turn left onto State Route 375. I point out the sign to Śakra. "That's the official name. In 1996 State Route 375 was renamed Extraterrestrial Highway. It runs alongside the north-eastern edge of Area 51. Rachel is forty-five minutes from here."

Amazing. Great for tourism, I'm sure.

After fifteen minutes we pass Groom Lake Road on the left and a few minutes later pull off next to Mailbox Road. "This is the famous Black Mailbox. UFO watchers like to gather here at night because it provides excellent views of the sky over Groom Lake."

That mailbox is white.

"Now it is white and bulletproof. It used to be black before it was upgraded."

Why don't we post a letter to Area 51 explaining that we are looking for the eleventh sacred object?

I smile. "My research indicates that the mailbox belongs to a local rancher in Tikaboo Valley."

Baset circles the mailbox a few times then begins hissing and spitting. Ra steps in for a closer look. *Hmm ... A wonderful piece of innocuous surveillance technology. Wonder what they'll find when they run me through the database.*

"Really?" I turn my back on the box. "That dirt road leading south is called Mailbox Road. It intersects with Groom Lake Road which leads to the main gate of Area 51."

The sun-god folds his arms and grins. *Considering they have already seen us, we may as well take a trip down that road.*

"Are you crazy? What happened to stealth and secrecy?"

He puts a finger to his lips and jumps into the 4x4. We hop in and I begin reluctantly driving. On the ridge I can see an SUV tracking our movements. The signs clearly say Restricted Area, No Trespassing, Use Of Deadly Force Authorised. I am feeling very uncomfortable.

We don't make it to the main gate. Camouflage-clad security personnel intercept us. Stern and polite, they order us to turn around. Ra gets out the car, puts his hands in the air and walks toward them. *Attention! I am from another world. Take me to your leader.*

I don't know whether to laugh or cry. Is he being serious?

A warning shot is fired. Suddenly Ra starts glowing. I reverse the vehicle a few metres. The heat emanating from him becomes intense. I hear the security requesting backup. No one moves. A black helicopter appears over the ridge. We hear instructions to keep still and wait for the Lincoln County Sheriff's Department.

A shock wave of light explodes from the sun-god. Everything goes dark; even with sunglasses I am blinded. Tires moving on gravel ... more vehicles ... hushed voices conferring ... we are loaded into an air-conditioned car.

By the time my sight returns we are driving through huge camouflaged doors in the side of a mountain. Once inside, soldiers escort us to a blue holding area where we are greeted by an officer. "They've been scanned for weapons, sir. All clear." Interesting. I can still feel my necklace.

Ra opens the discussion. *I am here to trade information. Your world is in imminent danger. And I need something from you.*

And so begins our life in Area 51. He had a plan after all.

Our access is understandably restricted. We are only allowed to travel in areas where Ra can contribute his advanced knowledge. There are many levels, sectors and corridors in Papoose Mountain. It is pointless moving without consulting a wall map. Subdermally-implanted microchips feed the central computer with the location of every person on the base; they also allow admission to authorised places.

In August I experience two shocks: The discovery of a transcontinental underground pod-transport system called the Heisenberg Train. Something to do with collapsing wave-functions and instantaneous travel. Also, the newsfeed is displaying images of the destruction of Punjab in India. An enormous earthquake has wiped out the entire city including the Golden Temple. It is heartbreaking to watch.

Later I begin wondering if these events are linked. Is Apophis trying to destroy the underground transport system? Or is he more interested in razing religious and sacred sites? Whatever his motive, it gives Ra increasing leverage at Area 51.

Scientists and engineers are assisting with the decoding of the Mezuzah. The scripture etched into its side makes reference to an ancient airship, or spacecraft, as they prefer to call it here. A month spent in the artefacts museum finally unearths a silver ring bearing a Hebrew inscription. Translated, it means Ring of Ezekiel. A bit more investigating reveals the switch to shrink it to necklace size. There is no doubt that this is the eleventh sacred object.

The only problem is that no one knows how to use it.

It is October. Ra is explaining how he has briefed the generals about Apophis and the dark ones. Black triangular Aurora X planes have been despatched to gather intelligence. New technologies are being developed. The sun-god is holding his head in his hands. *I am running out of information to trade. We need to solve the enigma of the Mezuzah.*

Enigma ... an enigmatic poem ... "The reading by Iboga!"

What?

"She said something like the Mezuzah is your only hope of getting home. I think those words were meant for you. Perhaps the Ring of Ezekiel is a transport device. Could it be an intergalactic version of the Loophole?"

His eyes light up. *Indeed!*

He pulls the Ring from his necklace and it reverts to natural size – silver, four metres in diameter and covered in strange inscriptions.

"That's not as easy to wield as the Loophole."

Ra is searching across the symbols. *Here it is. The hole in the shape of a six-pointed star. This must be how you activate it. How did that poem go?*

I rub my eyebrow. "Um ... Turn each end and count to three, and soon you'll have a master key."

He picks up the Mezuzah from the table and gives it a few twists and turns, finally rotating each end in opposite directions. A glowing six-pointed three-centimetre-long key emerges. *Eureka!*

"Should we assume it works like the Loophole?"

You mean I can only go where I've been before? Why the limitation?

"The Heisenberg Train operator spoke about the observer's consciousness collapsing the wave-function." I rub my eyebrow again. "Śakra said that *You are consciousness and your intention directs your journey.*"

Are you trying to give me lessons in advanced quantum mechanics?

"I don't know. There is something burning in the back of my mind. I can't figure it out."

Ra inserts the key. The inside of the ring shimmers into a silver-blue. *Ok, I am thinking of my home.*

He steps through. Instantly both the sun-god and the Ring disappear. I wait for a few hours but he does not return. Perhaps it's a one-way ticket. I swallow hard. Our leverage has gone.

During November our activities are severely curtailed. Śakra and I ask about leaving the base but our requests are stonewalled. Baset becomes quite tetchy and only our softest words avert an attack on the guards. It seems that our value diminishes once we have nothing to offer.

We spend most of our time watching the newsfeed and pacing the corridors. In December another calamity strikes the earth. Huge portions of the west coast become submerged. Part of Oregon and most of California disappear into the ocean. Scientists are saying that the poles are shifting. They cannot predict the course.

I look at Śakra. "What are we still doing here? Ra is not coming back."

I know. I was thinking the same.

"May I operate the silver circle?"

You have a destination in mind?

I take it from him and throw it to the ground. The three of us jump through. We land at the Black Mailbox.

Why here? They'll come after us.

"With the poles shifting, the base will be under threat. They won't be worrying about us. And there is something I need to do."

We hitch a ride and continue our journey along the Extraterrestrial Highway toward Rachel. I point out another sign: Speed Limit Warp 7. The monk laughs. *They have obviously never heard of the Loophole or the Ring of Ezekiel.*

Within twenty minutes we are at the Little A'Le'Inn motel. I find the owner and apologise for not showing up in June. "We were … um … detained."

She smiles knowingly. "It's not the first time I've heard that. Don't worry, you paid upfront. No harm done. Would you like an alien burger?"

I nod. "Yes please, three double burgers, the third without the bun. And a room for the night."

"Room's on the house and burgers coming right up."

After dinner we peruse the alien souvenirs and I purchase two t-shirts. One for the Star Child: Speed Limit Warp 7. One for me: Use Of Deadly Force Authorised. We have a good laugh. Then it's quick showers and an exhausted sleep. I have the feeling tomorrow will be an early start.

* * *

When Śakra awakens he immediately says *We have to go to Oregon.*

"Isn't it underwater?"

Not all of it. Anyway, we'll soon find out.

Great. Next adventure: Pacific Ocean.

The motel breakfast is superb. Soon we are standing outside, silver circle in hand. I close my eyes in apprehension. The Loophole opens and we jump through.

I land on solid ground. There is water everywhere. "Where are we?"

Wizard Island, Crater Lake, Oregon.

"Cool name. What are we doing here?"

I want to check on the Klamath Tribes. It seems they now have ocean views.

"Native Americans?"

Yep. The Klamath Tribes are a confederation of the Klamath, Modoc and Yahooskin. They have a reservation in the basin of Klamath County.

Crater Lake is located in the Cascade Mountains; this is why we are surrounded by peaks.

"The scenery is spectacular. Reminds me of when we first met at Lake Manasarovar on Mount Kailash."

This is an equally sacred site to the Indians. The lake is 9.5 kilometres wide and 590 metres deep – the deepest lake in the United States – and was 1,880 metres above sea level before the poles shifted. The intense blue colour is a result of the sunlight penetrating deep into its remarkably clear water. Although Crater Lake National Park is under snow for many months of the year, the lake seldom freezes over. We are standing on Wizard Island which is located on the west side of the lake.

"What do we do now?"

We wait.

"Let me guess. A member of the Council of Light has been notified."

I think you're finally getting the hang of this.

"Will you tell them to bring lunch?"

Are you always hungry?

"Seems that way. Fast metabolism. Or maybe it's the stress. Do you think Apophis shifted the poles?"

I am unsure, but it is very likely.

"Shock and awe. An astute way to seize power."

Activate the Adi Shakti if you want to keep warm. I don't believe it will attract attention.

"Thanks. I'm freezing."

We walk around the island and the morning passes quickly. Later in the day a few of the Klamath join us. Jovial greetings and back-patting abound. We build a campfire and settle into the inevitable discussions. This time I am allowed to attend. I guess there must be some reason.

After an hour the medicine man makes an announcement. "Crater Lake has always been the location of our vision quests. Considering the dire state of the planet it would be good to do one together."

"How does it work?" I ask.

"We construct the sweat lodge this afternoon. The ceremony starts in the early evening when you sweat for two hours. After this you wash and change into fresh clothes. You then return to the lodge and spend the next four nights and three days 'crying for your sacred dream'. During this questing, a fire burns continually but you are not sweating. The entire process takes place in complete darkness and total silence."

"You are not part of the process?"

He looks at me like I am a child. "I will be holding the space and keeping the fire. Sometimes I will be drumming or chanting. I also ensure that there is plenty of water available."

We forgo sleep and food during the vision quest.

"The whole time?"

Yep. We will have a late lunch. Then it's only water.

I disguise my concern. "What are we trying to achieve?"

Focus your mind, heart and soul on receiving spiritual guidance and purpose. Insights about yourself and the world may come in the form of a vision.

The monk probably senses my reluctance. He leans in close and says in a hushed tone *This vision quest is a rite of passage. It marks your transition from adolescence to spiritual adulthood.*

"Oh."

The afternoon is busy and the food, when it arrives, most welcome. Soon we are ensconced in the smoky lodge. Nothing to do but think and breathe and dream. Moments of panic grip me but then I hear the soothing chanting. Hours blend into hours ... time disappears ... gazing through narrowing eyes ... got to stay awake ... hunger passes ... drumming spurs me on ... the teachings of the last five years ... where's it all going? ... how did I get here? ... my life has changed ... things are so different ...

The march of the women and children ... a distant memory? ... the future? ... who are we? ... why are we sitting complacently? ... the world needs us ... we are the world ... We the People ... yes ... We the People ... we hold these truths to be self-evident ... all humans are created equal ... endowed with unalienable rights ... Life, Liberty and the pursuit of Happiness ... it is up to us ... find our strength ... remember our power ... rise up and create a new world ... suffused with peace, freedom and loving-kindness ...

A luminous hummingbird ... what's it doing here? ... flitting and dancing near my face ... bringer of wisdom ... leader ... take on the mantle ... each person making a difference ... it's our planet ... we can take it back ... the earth mother grieves ... Gaia beckons ... rise up ... rise up!

The lodge door opens ... people stirring ... moving ... time to shake off the reverie ... throw water onto my face ... stumble out into the cold ... activate the Adi Shakti ... walking to the stone circle ... watching the magnificent sunrise ... feel so bonded ... something greater than all of us.

After a light breakfast we sleep until noon. Then we gather around the circle to enjoy another meal and share our experiences. The medicine man listens with great interest, providing interpretation and advice where necessary. Gradually the atmosphere takes on a more sombre mood. The Klamath elder says he has an important message.

"There is not much time," he informs us. "You must take this golden eagle feather to our brothers in South America. They will know what to do."

Śakra opens his hand and the elder places it in his palm. He stares at it thoughtfully. *What is the purpose of this feather? Why should I carry it?*

The Klamath Indians look carefully at each other. A tense pause. "It is one half of the twelfth sacred object."

The monk is frowning. *Why have you never shared this with me?*

"It was entrusted to us by our ancestors. Selected elders of each generation were sworn to secrecy and dedicated their lives to keeping it safe until the time of the prophecy. That time is now."

Which prophecy?

"The one about –"

Śakra, are you there? Adam?

It's Ra! His voice echoes through the Adi Shakti.

"Hey! Where are you? What happened?"

I went home. It worked perfectly. Considering we only have 18 months left in this cycle, I decided to bring reinforcements.

"Great! Where are you?"

In Peru, South America.

I glance at Śakra. Talk about timing. There's that feeling of divine orchestration again. Who's really in charge here?

Jump as soon as you can. I think 2029 is going to be a stormy year.

"Peru's a big place. You want to be more precise?"

The city of Iquitos in the Peruvian rainforest.

"I've been there before. See you soon."

The elder reaches over to Śakra. "Push the tip of the quill." He does so and immediately the feather shrinks to necklace size. The monk hands it to me. *I want you to carry it. It has something to do with uniting your world.*

His energy field has changed. I try to read him ... it's like watching a candle flame flickering precariously in a breeze.

He looks me in the eye. *Something is calling me. I feel my time here coming to an end.*

Gooseflesh crawls along my legs and my stomach flip-flops. "No, you're not going anywhere." I want to believe otherwise, but as the words leave my mouth I remember that the energy field always tells the truth.

I stare at the ground for a moment. "No."

He puts his arm around my shoulder. *Everyone dies. The question is: How did I live?*

"Mandu told me 'Your job is to bloom – for yourself and for the world'. I don't think your job is finished yet."

His face suddenly looks creased and tired. I have never seen him like this before. I stand and bow deferentially to the Klamath. "Do we have anything else to discuss?" They shake their heads. "Walk with purpose and leave no footprints."

I wink at Baset. With a deft move I place the Golden Feather onto my necklace and pluck the Loophole from his. Throwing it to the ground, I bundle us through. I have never seen the cat move that fast.

* * *

Iquitos, the largest city in the Peruvian rainforest. Situated on the left bank of the Amazon river. Abundant rainfall and hot temperatures all year round. Nice.

Baset starts a slow run. Śakra suggests we keep up with her. Within fifteen minutes we spot a familiar figure. The cat leaps into the waiting arms of Ra and nuzzles him affectionately.

He beams a smile. *Great to see you all!*

"I thought this country might be underwater."

The Andes mountain range has protected it from the rising Pacific. Iquitos is also about 900 kilometres inland.

"So what's the plan?"

Our 4x4 is parked along that road. We are going into the rainforest to meet the shamans.

Déjà vu all over again. Here I am driving into another adventure with a cat, a monk and a sun-god. I smile to myself. There has to be a joke in there somewhere.

We arrive at the jungle sanctuary. Wooden huts are scattered along a serene lagoon surrounded by lush foliage. The incessant clamouring of insects is counterpointed by the lively prattle of scarlet and blue-yellow macaws, green parrots and azure kingfishers.

Three shamans are waiting for us. The Star Child alights and greets everyone. Introductions follow.

I whisper to the monk. "What exactly is shamanism?"

Shamanism is an ancient philosophy and practice based on energy, freedom, unconditional love, compassion and an appreciation of the Mystery of Life. In its essence, shamanism involves energy healing and guidance through communication with the multi-dimensions. A practitioner of shamanism is known as a shaman (pronounced shah-men or shay-men). Shamans are adept at finding and returning hidden soul fragments, gathering and returning dispersed soul energy, and cleansing negative energy from the energy field.

"This is a whole other level ..."

Indeed. These shamans will be guiding you along your journey. Each one has a particular speciality: Palos, Sanango and Ayahuasca.

I look at him quizzically.

Adam, you are going to spend time with the palero. Please follow him.

I tread the path to the shaman's dwelling. He shows me where I will be sleeping and the location of the dining area and washroom.

"As long as you work with me, you will adhere to this diet: Green plantains, yucca meal, chicken, eggs, fish. No salt, sugar or oil. No alcohol, caffeine or nicotine."

Sounds yummy. "What is the reason for this?"

"To purify and devote your body to the particular plant you will be ingesting. The plant spirit recognises this sacrifice and infuses you with its medicine. The plant spirit is your teacher."

Plant spirits? Medicines? I sigh. Time to surrender and trust again.

For the next three months I am drinking teas made from the barks of various Amazonian medicinal trees. Each plant seems to have a cleansing and revitalising effect and my energy and enthusiasm seem boundless. I have not met any plant spirits. When I ask about this, he laughs. "Don't you know how to read energy? Everything is energy. Everything is spirit. Everything is consciousness."

I feel a bit silly. Have I missed something? Are these plants talking to me as their energy infuses mine? I have been focusing on the physical experience and the idea of medicine. Apparently these teas have been having a conversation with my soul. I promise to start paying more attention.

Śakra is chatting to me over dinner. *How's it going? Learning anything?*

"Looking beyond the surface. Peeking beneath the layers. The shaman doesn't talk much. He says that experience and insight are my greatest teachers."

You do realise that plants live across the multi-dimensions?

"Excuse me?"

Think about it. Are you a physical or spiritual being? Are you expressed only in one dimension?

I stare at my bland meal. "Are we interacting with energies from other dimensions?"

It is more precise to say that we are interacting with consciousness in many dimensions.

"Just when I am catching up, you stretch my mind a bit further."

The monk smiles. *Tonight you begin working with the sananguero.*

The sananguero is rather trenchant. "You will continue the diet of the palero. For one month you will drink a combination of Sanango root bark and water. This will take place every second evening next to that large twisting vine. Sanango is a potent medicine that facilitates deep cleansing and purging of dark and illness-producing energy."

The nights are beautiful and warm. The occasional hawk screeches overhead. Owls hoot from secret places while frogs sing a merry chorus. The jungle surges with a sensual vivacity. My mind sparkles lucidly and my emotions bubble ebulliently.

"This has prepared you for the ayahuasquero," he says one morning. "Take four days off. Relax. Integrate what you have learned. Do not stray from the diet."

It's amazing how my body has adapted. I sneak a mouthful of honey at breakfast and almost gag from the sweetness. I begin to wonder if we need so much sugar and salt in our meals. Perhaps sugar acts like an addictive drug. Or maybe it makes our bodies feel good when our emotions are low. All I know is that I feel mentally and physically vibrant.

I am watching the newsfeed in the dining room. Ra is sitting next to me. 'Breaking news: During the night fiery meteorites rained down upon Mecca and Medina, destroying both cities. This resulted not only in the catastrophic loss of human life but in the ruination of Islam's most holy sites. In a special interview the leader of the World Peace Organisation made this dramatic statement: "This is an omen. It is time to put aside the superstition of religion. Who ended poverty in Africa? Who united the Middle East? Was it God? No, it was Apophis. It is time to unite our world under one peaceful umbrella."'

What a terrible tragedy. But it's still not enough. He must declare his hand.

The ayahuasquero walks over. "Are you ready for the teacher plant? The next two months will involve an Ayahuasca journey every second night. The days between are for rest and recuperation."

My stomach tightens. "Could you brief me a little?"

"Ayahuasca is an entheogen, meaning it assists you to 'meet God within'. This Amazonian plant concoction has been used by South American shamans for thousands of years. Its various names include caapi, natema, mihi and yage. Ayahuasca is from the Quechua language and it means Vine of the Soul or Vine of the Spirit. Ayahuasca is actually a blend of the vine *Banisteriopsis caapi* (ayahuasca) and the psychoactive leafy plant *Psychotria viridis* (chacruna)."

"It's not that huge twisting vine, is it?"

"Yes, the one you have been leaning against for a month."

"Is this going to be a very different experience?"

He nods. "Ayahuasca is a powerful tea used for healing and transcendence. It is imperative that it is consumed only under the supervision of a shaman or spiritual guide. I will be with you during every journey and sometimes other shamans will be present. This will allow you to let go and experience profound learning and insight. The journeys take place in the maloka – the ceremonial hut – which provides a safe and sacred environment. Within forty-five minutes of drinking Ayahuasca you will begin to feel its effects and your journey will last about four to six hours. You will vomit, probably a few times, but this corresponds with the release of negative energy. We provide a bucket and tissues."

I am trembling slightly. Ok, try to keep calm …

"Ayahuasca often carries you into your dramas, buried traumas and shadows. Sometimes you experience scary visions and a feeling of dying. The secret is to surrender and not resist … breathe … be a witness to whatever is happening. You will gradually move through the darkness and arrive at beautiful visions, deep teachings and transcendence. There is no point chasing, fighting or analysing – just be with the flow of mystical experiences. This is the journey inward through the layers of your mind and soul toward the Light."

I settle into the routine. Every second night I down a shot glass of Ayahuasca and lay on a soft mattress in the ceremonial hut. The shaman forgot to mention that the body temperature drops occasionally, resulting in shivers. I learn to dress in layers.

The ayahuasquero sings icaros throughout the night, interspersed with periods of silence. These songs manage the spiritual aspects of the journey and provide a comforting support. He also uses a shacapa – a rattle made of bundled leaves – to direct positive energy and to cleanse and expel negative and dark energy.

The visions, when they arrive, are no hallucinations. This is the full immersion experience. I lose awareness of my surroundings and disappear into other realities. I am in the centre of an enormous high-speed film watching a kaleidoscope of earth's history and cultures ... now the entire spectrum of planetary wildlife sweeps before me, each animal morphing into the next one ... now I am looking down from high in the cosmos at everything that exists, as it swirls into a nebulous mass then gradually spirals upward into the finest point of light ... witnessing all existence returning to the Source ... now swimming deep in gorgeous cyan waters ... in the distance a woman with long auburn hair is calling me ... now drowning in beauty and light ...

Every night brings its fears and wonders.

One evening the Star Child and I are sitting on the rocking chairs staring out over the garden. A large iguana and a monkey stroll past. For a moment they stop and gaze at us. Are they together? Are they friends?

"What a bizarre –"

Did they enter our reality or did we enter theirs?

"What do you mean?"

The veil between the worlds is dissolving.

"I don't follow."

You will.

After a month of intense journeys I begin to realise that something profound and spectacular is happening. Amazing and confusing realities cross my path during the waking hours. Are these the multi-dimensions?

One morning I see a luminous hummingbird with green, silver and gold plumage. It hovers outside my bedroom then flits inside and dances around my face. A delicate voice whispers "Bring me the silver condor feather."

I rush to the dining room to tell Śakra. He looks pleased. *It must be on its way. The universe is right on schedule.*

A few days later I am walking in the forest, reflecting and pondering upon the numerous consciousness-shifting episodes. The ramble affords some precious solitude. To my surprise I stumble across an Indian sitting in a clearing. He is performing a ceremony with stones laid out on a colourful weaving.

"I have been waiting for you," he says. "Come sit with me."

He shows me seven engraved stones. "These are chumpi stones or kuyas, used for centuries by the Q'ero shamans for divination and healing. Each one connects to a sacred mountain. Each one carries a message. I gathered these kuyas from the Urubamba River near the Inca Trail."

"The path that leads to Machu Picchu?"

"The very same. The mountain of your destiny."

He reaches into his poncho, pulls out a feather and places it in my hand. I hold it up and watch it gleaming in the sunlight. The Silver Feather. I bow reverently then push the tip of the quill and add it to my necklace. When I look up he is gone.

The gentle whirring of hummingbird wings beckons me across the forest floor. I hurry back to the garden near the ceremonial hut and shout for the monk. He comes running, followed closely by Ra and Baset. After a brief discussion we gather the shamans.

We are sitting in a circle. I lay the Silver Feather and the Golden Feather on the grass. Within moments the hummingbird appears. It hovers intently before each one of us as if it is scanning our souls. Then it darts to the ground and begins weaving in a blinding blur of light. When it is finished, all that remains is a beautiful multi-coloured Rainbow Feather.

The twelfth sacred object. At last!

I hear the delicate whisper. "This feather is to unite your world. All people, all races, all colours, all creeds. Use it wisely. Carry it with you always."

The glowing feather makes its way around the circle. Finally the master shaman speaks. "It is time to fulfil the prophecy."

Śakra repeats the question he posed to the Klamath. *Which prophecy?*

"The ancient Inca prophecy which proclaims: 'When the Eagle of the North flies with the Condor of the South, The Spirit of the Land, She will Reawaken'. This refers not only to the unification of North and South America but to the blending of the heart, intuition and spiritual with the mind, rational and material."

Everyone is looking at me expectantly. What am I supposed to do? I close my eyes and read the energy of the sacred object. 'Hold me high above your head, let me feel the sun's caress, wave me three times in a circle, and get ready to be blessed.'

I raise the Rainbow Feather to the sky and follow the protocol. The shamans are holding a clear intention. I call out "Unite the Americas!" We sit in silence for a while.

Two weeks later the newsfeed carries an interesting story: 'June 2029 will go down in history as the month the American Peace Organisation was established. It will be formally ratified on the 7th of July during the signing of the Peace Accord at the White House. After three years of discussions and negotiations, North and South America have agreed to share resources, information and technology to empower and develop both continents. What we are seeing is the beginning of a true United America.'

On July 1ˢᵗ Apophis appears on the newsfeed, presenting himself as the de facto leader of a United Europe, Middle East and Africa. He ridicules the APO as a poor imitation of the WPO, saying that they will never achieve the loyalty he commands. He fails to mention the political leaders who were removed from power and replaced by dark ones.

On July 7ᵗʰ, perhaps to upstage the positive news from America, Apophis gives an interview: "Religion is an antiquated pointless superstition that severely hinders peace and progress. Advanced technology, knowledge-sharing and humanitarian ethics are what build strong and prosperous countries. Today I issued a decree banning all religions and religious practices in United Europe, Middle East and Africa. Demolition of holy sites and sacred buildings will begin immediately. Uprisings will be severely quelled."

Ra stands up and Baset leaps from his arms. Walking outside, he removes the sparkling Staff of Light from his necklace and raises it high in the air. Twelve lightning bolts streak from the pine cone into the heavens. He slams the base of the staff into the ground and declares gravely: *The final countdown begins.*

He looks across at Śakra and me. *Say your goodbyes. We leave in the morning.*

Dinner is a curious mix of jubilance and solemnity. I express my deep gratitude to these shamans who practice the ancient and mystical jungle arts. A memory flashes in my mind: An iguana and a monkey strolling across the garden. I have to laugh. The shamans, the sultry rainforest and the plant spirits have all been great teachers.

* * *

Machu Picchu at dawn. There is nothing like it. We watch as the first sunrays peer over the horizon. The time-worn ruins look mysterious and spectacular in the soft yellow light. Magnificent mountain heads guard the sacred expanse of stone buildings and grass steps.

We're going to be here a long time. Baset has found a hotel about a hundred metres from the entrance. You need to go book every available room for one year.

"An entire year?"

Yes. Take Śakra with you.

We stroll down the mountain path and locate the Machu Picchu Sanctuary Lodge. Fortunately the owner is present and we manage to negotiate rooms and meals for twelve months. It will cost every last diamond so I hope Ra knows what he is doing.

Considering that we just about own the place, we get a tour of our new home. Two suites and twenty-nine rooms, twelve of them with a stunning view of the mountains. As the current occupants leave over the next few weeks, we will gradually take over the entire hotel.

We walk through the hotel gardens, lingering to admire the many orchids, then finally relax on the terrace. *Feel like some breakfast?*

"Thought you'd never ask."

The waiter brings a menu featuring international cuisine and Andean specialities. We ask him about the weather. He explains that every day is the same, usually a warm 25 degrees Celsius, with rain during the summer months. I smile and stretch my legs. Sounds perfect.

"What do you think Ra is planning?"

I am unsure. We'll find out soon.

During breakfast I notice a hummingbird hovering over the nearby flowers.

"That plumage looks familiar. Reminds me of the sweat lodge at Crater Lake and the jungle in Iquitos."

As it should. It's the same hummingbird. It is your power animal.

"Power animal?"

Your guardian spirit and guide.

"I have a guardian spirit?" A small cloud casts a shadow over the table. "Why not a jaguar or an eagle?"

Count your blessings. The hummingbird is the sacred symbol of the shamans, as it is the only animal said to have seen the face of God.

"Wow. How did that happen?"

That is a most interesting question.

"And ...?"

It alights on my arm and gazes into my eyes. Sweet and disconcerting at the same time.

Try to stroke the feathers.

I move my other hand and it passes through the bird.

"What the –"

Śakra rolls up with laughter.

"How can it be solid on my arm but untouchable?"

You still don't get it, do you?

"Is this to do with coexisting realities?"

Yes.

"Am I experiencing the hummingbird in two realities?"

You've asked this question before.

I recall the conversation with Ra just prior to him jumping through the Ring of Ezekiel. And the iguana and the monkey strolling across the garden. And the Indian in the rainforest.

"It is more precise to say that we are interacting with consciousness in many dimensions."

My words exactly. What do they mean?

"Uh … the teacher plants … the shamanic exercises … meditation … these have been opening my consciousness to other realities … the multi-dimensions … once a veil has fallen the connection is permanently open … hence, you can only travel to where you've been before!"

What took you so long?

"I just couldn't put the pieces together."

When the doors of perception are cleansed …

"Am I already everywhere?"

Of course.

"What is stopping the rest of the veils from falling?"

Your mind. Your beliefs. They act as a filter, limiting your perception of All That Is.

"So I don't need the shamanic exercises?"

Only if you believe you do.

I push my fingers against my temples. Oh my ... it's too much to process. The whirring of hummingbird wings around my ears. The green trees and bright flowers colourfully expanding. Everything moving in slow motion. Waves of nausea squeeze my stomach. I grip the chair tightly. A shock wave of light bursts inside me. I am standing in the Vortex of Life. Reaching out, running my fingers along the spiralling doors, making the leap, entering and exiting, entering and exiting, entering and exiting.

The sun is high in the sky when I return to my reality. I am sprawled on the ground again. The monk is enjoying a cup of tea.

"I don't understand what is going on!" I cry out in frustration.

Yes, you do.

"Tell me!"

You are consciousness and your intention directs your journey.

He gets up and walks away, leaving me with a myriad thoughts. I spend the rest of the afternoon staring at the flowers and conversing with the hummingbird. There is no sound. No one disturbs me. I am alone.

If everything is happening at once, right here, right now, then I am at the centre of All That Is. There is nowhere to go and nothing to do. There are no veils nor doors, merely the shifting of my consciousness. I blink a few times. That's it!

I jump realities without moving, then do it again and again and again.

I say you are free.

Long white hair and piercing almond-shaped blue eyes are gazing upon me. Shimmering peaceful energy radiates through me. "Who are you?"

You are Life itself pulsating in every dimension. I say You are Free!

I am alone once more. The sunset is creating a gorgeous interplay of light and shadow. Pink and gold cascade across the sky. Leaves are tinted in maroon and vermilion. Birds chirp softly in the cool night air.

Eventually I stumble past the dining area and find my room. Collapsing on the bed, I enter another reality. A peaceful escape from an overwhelming and beautiful day.

* * *

I want to introduce you to someone Ra says one morning.

Standing in front of me is a man wearing a poncho and a brightly coloured hat. It's the Indian from the Iquitos rainforest.

The Q'ero are the direct descendants of the Inca. These shamans usually live very high in the Andes mountains. They are known as the Keepers of the Ancient Knowledge. Meet Shaman Chuya.

I nod respectfully and get a beaming smile in return.

You are going to be spending time with him.

"And you?"

I am monitoring Apophis and planning a war.

Chuya and I spend the next few weeks communing with the mountain and nature spirits of Machu Picchu. He is not much of a talker. It has taken me a long time to realise that those who speak the most usually know the least. When you have direct experiences with the Light and touch the sacred knowledge and power, you don't need to 'sell' it to anyone and you don't need to prove it to anyone. You have arrived and you know it. Your energy speaks far more than your words ever will.

As if to drive this point home, one afternoon the shaman stoops to pick up a shrivelled flower. Holding it in his palms he breathes over it three times. I watch in awe as the flower regenerates. This is his only explanation:

"The Q'ero are the masters of the living energy. As you know, everything is consciousness and everything is energy. We are energy beings interacting in an energy world. The secret is to keep your energy clear. Live the impeccable life. Walk in peace with the world. Accept what is, change what you can. Love unconditionally. Let go of judgements. Operate with radical respect to all living beings. You understand the Inca laws?"

I shake my head.

"In the Inca language, Quechua, the laws are called Munay, Llankay and Yachay. Munay refers to universal and unconditional love – an appreciation for all of creation. Llankay refers to living in service – actions of kindness, forgiveness and gratitude toward all of creation. Diligent practise of Munay and Llankay leads to Yachay, which refers to authentic inner knowing and higher consciousness – understanding your true nature."

It reminds me of the Sikh's mentorship toward exemplary character, the imam's teaching about good deeds and the Ubuntu philosophy of the sangoma. It is obvious that spiritual maturity is the gateway to stepping into the worlds of energy and power. This is why initiations and impeccability tests exist.

"You have one more lesson to learn."

"I do?"

"Yes. It is the hardest and most beautiful of all."

"It must be Love."

"You read my energy."

"Indeed. Tomorrow I commence my final journey."

He nods sagely.

We spend the rest of the day meditating and exchanging energy with the apus, the spirits of the Machu Picchu and Huayna Picchu mountains. My energy field is a butterfly dancing across the grass steps. I am filled with tremendous clarity and deep understanding. Gratitude and appreciation flow through me in peaceful waves.

* * *

We are sitting at the Temple of the Sun under a cloudless sapphire sky. It is a crisp morning and the birds are sweetly welcoming the new day.

The shaman is unpacking a number of stones and crystals and placing them onto his colourful weaving in a particular way. I notice that the centre of the design comprises a line of hearts. "These are my power objects," he says, "and when they are laid out on this manta cloth, the whole thing is called a mesa."

"Are you going to teach me about Love?"

"That can only be learned through experience."

"Oh." I wonder what we are doing here.

"And with a little help from the San Pedro teacher plant."

I was not expecting this. "Is it as challenging as Ayahuasca?"

"San Pedro is an ancient, sacred and magical mescaline cactus. It has been used for thousands of years by the shamans and healers of Peru as a way to facilitate powerful awakening, insight, learning and healing. Its various names are Cactus of Vision, Huachuma, El Remedio (the remedy) and San Pedro (alluding to Saint Peter holding the keys to heaven). Unlike Ayahuasca, San Pedro journeys take place during the day and you seldom vomit. It is usually a gentle journey that gradually immerses you in Love."

"That's a relief. Sounds more enjoyable."

"Within forty-five minutes of drinking San Pedro you will begin to feel its effects, and your journey will last about seven to nine hours. Part of you will be fully present with normal awareness while another part of you will have profound psychological, emotional and spiritual experiences. Are you ready to drink?"

I nod apprehensively. The shaman closes his eyes, says a prayer to Father Sky and Mother Earth and dedicates the event to peace, healing and love. He hands me a tall glass of green liquid, telling me to drink it quickly and take a few slow deep breaths. It tastes of earth, watermelon and mild ginger – quite palatable – but the texture is smooth and lumpy, like drinking raw eggs mixed with fruit juice. I try to keep my face composed.

Within thirty minutes I burst into tears and sob like never before. Unending rivers of grief and sadness flow out of me. Then a flood of insight ... no visions and no words ... just a *knowing* ... a complete understanding of myself, my patterns, my history and my relationships. And that's just the first two hours of the journey.

My senses heighten until they become acute. I hear the subtlest sounds and pick up scents far beyond the 'normal' human range. This must be a return to my natural state ... perhaps my senses have dulled from modern living. Soon I am swimming in the energy of the surrounding plant life ... engaging in silent conversation ... appreciating each distinctive quality and character ... enthralled by the flutter of hummingbird wings in the gentle breeze ...

I lay on my back and watch ethereal beings drift rapturously across the sky. A matrix of divine light appears behind them ... a sacred geometry ... everything arising from and receding into an awesome cosmic canvas ...

The smallest touch on my skin creates waves of expansive pleasure. Pulses of joy are surging through my entire being ... my soul becomes a cool fire ... thoughts and words disappear ... I am engulfed in Light ... overwhelmed with Love ... swept into an astounding orgasm of the Heart ...

"Wow," is all I manage to say at the end.

We watch the sunset, then walk back to the hotel for dinner. As expected, I'm starving. Ironically my appetite for 'heavy' food has diminished. I manage to eat only soup and salad before excusing myself and crawling into bed.

For three months I journey into Love. It is a powerful healer and teacher. I sense the connectedness of all things and finally understand the philosophy of the Q'ero. My gratitude toward Shaman Chuya is immense.

My profound experiences are bizarrely juxtaposed with the almost daily atrocities pouring through the newsfeed. Apophis has forbidden all religious and spiritual expression, and is decimating the religious populations within his jurisdiction. At the same time, countries falling under the WPO are enjoying unprecedented peace, health and prosperity. It's a clever strategy. Follow Apophis and you gain the world but lose your soul.

United America is reluctant to intervene because of Apophis' technological prowess and power, and the strong possibility of a world war. The Far Eastern countries also watch carefully from the sidelines.

What's the lesson here? asks Ra, after another terrible event on the newsfeed.

"If you play with fire, you will burn your fingers."

You read that in my energy.

"Yes, but what does it mean?"

This planet has walked on the dark side for too long. The orchestration of political and economic events; the constant flow of resources to a select minority; the sham of democracy; the pollution and destruction of the natural environment; the cruelty and profiteering of war; the hiding of spiritual truth. Yet the people of this world have the same desires: freedom, peace, prosperity, love, joy and connection to the Source.

The question is: Why are the gods watching and waiting?

"We the People need to find our power, take responsibility and rise up together. We are the ones who must bring change to the world."

True.

I sense there is something more. "The fire ...?"

The dark side always takes more than it gives. That's its nature.

Aha. The crux of the matter.

If the people of this earth play with fire, they will eventually get burned. The dark masters and the dark lattice were simply another step down the road of darkness. Apophis is showing you the ultimate destination of darkness: suffering and aloneness. Apophis is the last great teacher on your planet.

"Wow, that's a radical statement."

When will your world complete this lesson? At what point do the gods intervene?

"Are you asking me?"

Make sure you are at the Temple of the Sun on Friday at 8am.

"Why? What's happening?"

The meeting of the gods and the Council of Light for the summer solstice.

"I'll be there."

Later over dinner I wonder to myself: Did he say 'gods', as in the plural?

* * *

21 December 2029. The day of the summer solstice. A big event and I am running late. Can't understand it ... missed the wake-up call ... shower wasn't working ... one of those days I guess.

I walk up the pathway and around the corner. No one. I peer down the grass steps. Gathered around a solitary tree below the Temple of the Sun are a crowd of people. Where did they all come from? I spot the Sikh ... then the imam. There's the abbot and the Aboriginal elder. Further scrutiny reveals the sangoma ... the Hopi mystic ... the Klamath elder ... the Q'ero shaman ...

How many people make up the Council? Was it twelve? I count on my fingers. There must be another four members. Perhaps they represent the major religions and spiritual beliefs.

I hurry down and join everyone.

Ra raises his eyebrow. *The grand entrance of Adam Kadmon.* He motions me to sit next to Śakra, then continues:

From 9.12am you will conduct unceasing prayer, meditation, chanting and other energy practices right here in the centre of Machu Picchu. Stay in contact with your religious orders and tribes and ensure that they do the same. It is crucial that we bathe this world in enormous waves of positive energy for the next six months.

"And what are you going to do?"

We are going to war with Apophis.

166

"We?"

He opens his palms to the left and right. *The nine gods of light: Hathor, Shu, Tefnut, Geb, Nut, Osiris, Isis, Seth and Nephthys.*

That explains the unusual-looking beings standing next to Ra. "The ones you created? They actually exist?"

Of course.

Am I the only one who is surprised here? "Are these the reinforcements you spoke about when you arrived back on earth a year ago?"

Yes.

"Is this the foretold 'return of the gods'?"

Indeed.

"I thought there were originally many gods on earth. Are there only ten of you?"

Many legends in many cultures, same gods. And don't forget the Watchers. That makes twelve. Plus there is Apophis, his deputies Sek and Mot, and another nine dark lieutenants.

That makes twelve … and twelve … and twelve members of the Council of Light … and twelve sacred objects. What's so special about the number twelve?

Also there are many demi-gods on both sides … but that's a whole other story.

"What have your gods been doing for an entire year?"

Collecting information, gathering intelligence and fulfilling a lot of prophecies. There's been a few skirmishes too.

"Why didn't you tell me what was going on?"

You had your own journey to complete.

The energy field changes. I read the heightened anticipation. It must be a few minutes until 9.12am. I suddenly realise how significant the solstice must be to the sun-god.

In a moment the sun will reach its lowest annual altitude in the sky. The word solstice is derived from the Latin sol meaning 'sun' and sistere meaning 'to stand still'. It is the pause before the new cycle. It is the moment we declare war on Apophis. It marks the final showdown between light and darkness.

Everyone goes quiet. Ra points the Staff of Light toward the sun. He is glowing brightly. A terrific streak of light hits the pine cone, causing its scales to become white hot. He plants the base of the staff into the ground and announces: *May the Light bring forth the Golden Age.*

Immediately a serene chant begins. Gradually it becomes louder until it resonates through the stone ruins. White robes settle into prayer. Saffron robes begin meditating. I notice now that there are more than twenty-four people here. It seems that each spiritual leader has brought four devotees. The waves of energy emanating from the group are extraordinarily beautiful.

Ra opens the Ring of Ezekiel and the gods step through. Perhaps they have gone to a secret location where the airships are docked. Maybe they are strategically positioning themselves around the planet. Who knows?

As for me, I sit down under the tree to meditate. The energy is divine and it's a way I can contribute to the world. One thing's for sure: The hotel is going to be full tonight.

* * *

There is a war going on. For once, the newsfeed is reporting on real issues. Probably because they don't have a choice. The people of the world only have to look up to see the truth. A battle rages in the heavens. The skies are populated with military planes belonging to various nations, unmarked spacecraft from Area 51, and the airships of the gods. Shock and awe swirl across the globe.

A deluge of inescapable questions. 'Who are these beings? If extraterrestrials exist, what does this mean for our religions? What is missing in our history? Why has the truth been hidden? Who is in control of our world?'

The astonishment and confusion deepen on February 14th when Apophis declares himself to be the Dark Lizard. He says he intends to rule the world and eventually all will bow down and serve him. The dark ones installed in political, business and religious offices throughout the planet are subsequently revealed.

The Council of Light – the true spiritual leaders of the world – motivate and mobilise their followers. The earth is filled with prayer, meditation, chanting, dancing and multifarious sacred ceremonies. I work with the shamans and elders to master the multi-dimensions. My days are a blur of spectacular sunrises and mystical moonlit nights.

During the month of May something incredible happens. Women and children start marching in the streets of every country. The newsfeed shows an almighty collaboration of feminine power.

Banners reflect emphatic messages: 'Enough!' ... 'Time for Peace and Love' ... 'No more!' ... 'We the People'.

I get a lump in my throat and my heart feels warm. I am so proud of them. We are working together at last. People around the world waking up, taking a stand, contributing in whatever way they can. The gods have been waiting a long time for this.

I am watching the newsfeed with great interest. There is a huge demonstration in South America. Cameras zoom in on the leader ... passionate and earnest ... long auburn hair ... radiant blue eyes ... I scrutinise the hologram then shout to Śakra. "Come here! Quickly, quickly! Look, it's her. The woman in my vision."

He smiles. *Perfect timing.*

Messages coming in from Ra report that the dark ones are slowly being annihilated. The joint forces of the earth and the gods are turning the tide. The multi-pronged strategy of spiritual dedication, demonstrations and marches, and war on the ground and in the heavens is proving successful.

In June the Ring of Ezekiel shimmers on the lawn. Ra and Baset burst through, appearing unkempt, flustered and on edge. He hurriedly gathers the Council.

There is not much time. Apophis has discovered your location. You are a prime target.

My stomach tenses and my legs suddenly feel heavy. It is much easier to meditate than fight on the front lines.

Śakra takes the lead. Standing in the centre of the circle, he drops to one knee and grips his temples. One by one, the spiritual leaders do the same. I watch in fascination as white light spirals above every head. Dazzling beams begin to crisscross the sky, forming an enormous twelve-pointed star that covers the entire ruins.

I am astounded. "What's happening?"

The sun-god whispers: *Crystal skulls.*

I tap my head. "The Council members have crystal skulls?"

Yes. Each crystal skull allows communication with other crystal skulls and with the gods. They also give direct access to the multi-dimensions.

"Does Śakra have one?"

Of course. As do all the gods.

"Why am I always the last person to know?"

On the contrary, Adam, you are the first.

"Oh." I stare at the grass verge.

Now we wait.

Within the hour, three airships throw Machu Picchu into deep shadow.

Apophis, Sek and Mot. They've come alone.

I swallow hard. The energy field shifts. Such coldness. Desolation. Without warning, I am plucked into one of the multi-dimensions. It must be all the training … I can see the Council of Light from high above … yet I am walking through a dark mist at the same time. Śakra appears beside me. *You going somewhere?*

"What are you doing here?"

He smiles reassuringly. *You're not having your final adventure without me.*

There is a terrible noise below. I recognise the wild screech of Baset. We watch the flurry of gleaming claws and fangs as she disappears into a dark cloud. Across the other side of the ruins Ra is battling amid a salvo of shadowy blasts. Śakra despatches the Phoenix and it deftly destroys two of the ships before being blown out of the sky.

They are battling Sek and Mot. That must mean –

Greetings, monk. The deep timbre of the voice causes gooseflesh down my back and arms. He has no discernible face. I am staring into a stark abyss of darkness. *Adam, I presume.*

His laughter is chilling. *Do you know how much I enjoyed terminating the Guardian of the Earth? What great pleasure.*

The Star Child remains quiet. I apprehensively wait for the first move. The energy shield! My fingers creep toward the necklace. Apophis levels his hands at me and sneers. *I wouldn't bother. Your death is imminent. The question is: Why are you even living?*

I think back to the Aboriginal elder. "My job is to bloom – for myself and for the world."

Is it really? What's so special about you? You're just another pawn in the game. Your life is small and meaningless.

"What has meaning got to do with anything?"

You come from nothing and you return to nothing. You're a piece of cosmic dust.

"Not true. I arise from the Source and I return to the Source."

Life is futile and purposeless. Everything you build will be demolished. Everything you gain will eventually be lost. Why make the effort?

"All of life fundamentally comes down to a choice. I know which direction I am travelling. Do you?"

You stupid flea! Your insignificant life is about to end. What's it all been for?

I pause and gaze at my feet. Apophis is supposed to be the last great teacher. Why is he trying to instil fear and doubt in me? Without thinking, I touch the Koan. What was the message? 'One Cannot Grasp Water In A Closed Hand'

My mind leaps to the Cortile della Pigna at Vatican City. Ra said *The water flowing beneath the statue represents the flow of Life, the flow of creation. The manifestation of the unmanifested Creative Life Force.* Water is Life.

I recall Śakra teaching me about Tantra. *Pain and fear. Those dark emotions close hearts and corrupt relationships.* The Closed Hand is pain and fear. What else did he say? *Courage. Forgiveness. Vulnerability.*

In this unguarded moment I hear a loud scchhh! A dreadful crackle envelops me. It's too late to do anything. I look up in fright. The monk is standing before me. He collapses to the ground.

"Śakra!" I scream. A memory flickers. The words of Iboga. 'One of you will die for love. One of you will be sorely tempted. One of you will be seriously injured.'

I grab the monk and hold him in my arms. "Did you jump in front of me? Are you crazy?"

He smiles. *I owed you for saving my life.*

"Please don't die."

Your training is complete. My time is done. The Guardian is waiting for me. He signals with his eyes, indicating the necklace. My vision is clouding with tears. What is it? He signals again. I slip the Dart into my palm. He gasps and his body slumps.

Your death is inevitable, Adam. There is nothing to live for. Pain, fear, emptiness - that's all there is. All there ever will be.

I will not succumb. Not after all that Śakra has taught me. Not after everything we have shared.

Surrender to the pain. Why bother living? Why? Why? Why?

I feel the Dart in my hand. An irresistible force. Apophis closes the gap as if to embrace me. I remain stooped over the monk. At the last possible moment I hurl the diamond needle.

"I choose Life. I choose Light. And I choose Love!"

Apophis staggers in shock. Tries to level his arms. I activate the Adi Shakti. Plumes of light mingle with the darkness. I hear the crackle and brace myself. Instead, an almighty golden-white pulse explodes within the Dark Lizard. I shield my eyes from the Light. He is gone.

I scan the ruins. The sun-god is holding a shivering woman in his arms. I switch realities. "Ra, are you alright? What happened?"

Baset is wounded.

"Where is she?"

This is Baset. In her less-favoured form. She is also known as the goddess Tefnut.

I place my hand on his shoulder. "She is going to be fine. Do you remember the sangoma's reading? Well, I was tempted … and Śakra has left this world."

The sun-god is tearful. *It's been a long journey for the Star Child. He has fulfilled his mission admirably. He is now reunited with his true love.*

"It's been a long journey for all of us. The people of this planet have suffered enough."

Indeed. The 7-year cycle is complete. The dark lattice is broken. It is the dawn of the Golden Age.

"A new era of truth, freedom, peace, love and light."

I look up at the smoky sky. So many thoughts and emotions are surging through me. Losing Śakra is hard; it's going to hurt for a long time. Baset was a goddess all along. Darkness has been wiped from the earth. People around the globe are demanding change.

"Will you be leaving soon?"

The gods will stay until the earth is back on its feet. We will assist in the rebuilding and restructuring of your planet. Power and governance will remain firmly in the hands of humans.

I pat the dust from my clothes and stride over to the Council. The energy field is interesting. They have witnessed everything. They know what happened and where we are headed. I rest against the solitary tree and enjoy the serene ambience. My leadership is an unspoken reality. Words serve no purpose.

Eventually the Sikh intones: "What now, Adam?"

"A woman is waiting for me. Long auburn hair, radiant blue eyes and a beautiful smile."

I place my hands over my heart and nod reverently to the group. "And then, my friends, we have work to do. We are going to build a whole new world."

Nine sacred objects glimmer on my necklace. The Tantra Stone and the Rainbow Feather sparkle as reminders of the new era. I finally understand the Koan. One cannot grasp Life without courage, forgiveness and vulnerability.

As the Star Child once said: *This life is an Adventure of the Heart. It is not about power and greed and self-serving interests. It is about entanglement in reality – real people, unguarded hearts, deep connections. It's about sharing and visioning and holding hands. It's about vulnerability before each other and surrender before the Mystery.*

The blood-red sun is touching the horizon, painting the sky in crimson and mauve. A soft breeze flutters the grass. Birds are murmuring and gently nuzzling in the trees. Unusually, a full moon is mystically rising and splashing silver across the stone ruins. It's going to be a spectacular evening.

Stephen Shaw's Books

Visit the website: www.i-am-stephen-shaw.com

I Am contains spiritual and mystical teachings from enlightened masters that point the way to love, peace, bliss, freedom and spiritual awakening.

Heart Song takes you on a mystical adventure into creating your reality and manifesting your dreams, and reveals the secrets to attaining a fulfilled and joyful life.

They Walk Among Us is a love story spanning two realities. Explore the mystery of the angels. Discover the secrets of Love Whispering.

The Other Side explores the most fundamental question in each reality. What happens when the physical body dies? Where do you go? Expand your awareness. Journey deep into the Mystery.

Reflections offers mystical words for guidance, meditation and contemplation. Open the book anywhere and unwrap your daily inspiration.

5D is the Fifth Dimension. Discover ethereal doorways hidden in the fabric of space-time. Seek the advanced mystical teachings.

Star Child offers an exciting glimpse into the future on earth. The return of the gods and the advanced mystical teachings. And the ultimate battle of light versus darkness.

The Tribe expounds the joyful creation of new Earth. What happened after the legendary battle of Machu Picchu? What is Christ consciousness? What is Ecstatic Tantra?

The Fractal Key reveals the secrets of the shamans. This handbook for psychonauts discloses the techniques and practices used in psychedelic healing and transcendent journeys.

Lightning Source UK Ltd.
Milton Keynes UK
UKOW05f0718170317
296837UK00001B/54/P